Presented To:

_____

From:

_____

Date:

_____

LIVING
Isaiah 54

LIVING

Isaiah 54

YOUR MAKER IS YOUR HUSBAND

DISCOVERING THAT YOUR HEAVENLY FATHER WANTS NOTHING SHORT OF A PASSIONATE, LOVING, SOUL-MATE RELATIONSHIP WITH HIS SONS AND DAUGHTERS

MARY ELLIOTT

DESTINY IMAGE® PUBLISHERS, INC.
P.O. Box 310, Shippensburg, PA 17257-0310
"Promoting Inspired Lives."

This book and all other Destiny Image, Revival Press, MercyPlace, Fresh Bread, Destiny Image Fiction, and Treasure House books are available at Christian bookstores and distributors worldwide.

For a U.S. bookstore nearest you, call 1-800-722-6774.
For more information on foreign distributors, call 717-532-3040.
Reach us on the Internet: www.destinyimage.com.

ISBN 13 TP: 978-0-7684-4052-2
Ebook 13 ISBN: 978-0-7684-8884-5

For Worldwide Distribution, Printed in the U.S.A.
1 2 3 4 5 6 7 8 9 10 11 / 13 12

Endorsement

Mary Elliott has written a book of encouraging counsel for struggling women from one who has been there. She offers a personal perspective that's generously sprinkled with Scripture and tender references to the many facets of our loving God and Redeemer. Her insight came from painful experiences that drove her to the steadfast, unfailing love of her Savior, the source of all things. She urges wounded souls, both married and single, to embrace forgiveness and to serve others from the heart.

—Marilyn Gregory, former assistant manager with
LifeWay Christian Stores
and author of *Warming Trends*

CONTENTS

DEDICATION

First and foremost, thanks and praise be to the Father, Son, and Holy Spirit.

This book is for all the men and women who have felt abandoned or forsaken at one time or another. The Father's heart is to let you know that He is your husband, your friend, your source, and your healer always.

Also, to my wonderful parents, who still, though they are both with our Father in Heaven, live on in my life.

I also dedicate this to my children, Brent and KC. I am so blessed that Father gave you to me to raise. You help to inspire me! May God bless you and keep you.

And finally, to the many who helped me with this book. I'm reluctant to name them for fear of leaving one out. However, I must try.

To Jennifer, for your countless hours of insightful editing—thank you.

To Deborah, for your lovely artwork and inspired poetry—thank you.

To Rabbi Moshe, his wife Dr. Martha, and James, for taking the time out of your busy schedules to allow me an interview—thank you.

To Bonnie and Riley, for helping to fulfill prophecy and pointing the way—thank you.

To my brothers, sisters, and friends in the Lord, Terry, Toni, Chris, Vina, Sonja, David, Nina, Pam, Tony, Myron, Kathy, and Ro—your prayers and help cannot be measured.

To Pastor Don LaBrot and his wife, Gale, for allowing the Holy Spirit to lead and saying just the right words at just the right time.

To my publishing company, editors, and book agent, Marti, thanks for your help and encouragement in putting wings to this ministry.

Finally, to all the rest who prayed, listened, and gave advice (you know who you are)—so many thanks for your encouragement, your prayers, and your help. It is as the Word says in Psalm 142:7, *"The righteous shall surround me, for You shall deal bountifully with me."* He surely has.

INTRODUCTION

"So, you're an Isaiah 54 woman!" I proclaimed over the phone. I had just prayed with a dear, hurting, soon-to-be single woman, "Thy Maker is thine Husband." As we finished the prayer, I told her she was an Isaiah 54 woman.

"What does that mean?" she asked.

"Oh, you know, when I prayed with you and said, *'Your Maker is your Husband,'* and also when I said, *'No weapon formed against you shall prosper'*—those are both out of Isaiah 54. Oh, and by the way, I'm an Isaiah 54 woman too." Being a divorced mother with two small children, I *knew* this passage.

She said she would write that down and look it up. We said, "God bless you" to each other and then our good-byes. After I hung up the phone, I pondered that proclamation I had made to her for days. I had prayed it for others too. I am a prayer partner with a local Christian television station. I go into that station's prayer room and pray for people all over the country about their daily battles and struggles with life. But that day it hit me. I realized that most of us *are* Isaiah 54 men and women. Actually, I'm surprised that more people haven't already discovered this chapter. Of course people know it exists, but I mean really *know* this chapter out of Isaiah. I have lived it, breathed it, wondered it, cried it, and proclaimed it, and I pray that it speaks to you as well.

All of us can claim this for ourselves. Who of us doesn't need someone to take care of us from time to time? Or all the time? Thankfully, *we have* that someone. He is our Father God, our provider, our strength and help in times of trouble, our fortress, our deliverer, our Redeemer, our rock, our high tower, our King of kings and Lord of lords, our Daddy God, and our Husband. Praise God!

My declaration over this precious woman also started me thinking about the Proverbs 31 woman, and I pondered that passage for days, too. Proverbs 31:10 says *"Who can find a virtuous wife?"* I knew I was a virtuous wife when I was married. Loyalty has always had the highest priority on my list, and I was that—loyal to the bone. I was brought up that way. Even if my husband (at the time) wasn't, I was loyal and would always be. In my way of thinking, two wrongs didn't make a right. I had that one down.

The Tanach translation of Proverbs 31:10 reads, *"An accomplished woman who can find?"* As a single person, I was running a successful farming operation, was an accomplished horseback rider, and worked other seasonal jobs when the farming season was slow. I thought I had it all at the time.

As we read further in Proverbs 31, we see that it describes a rich, married woman—mega-rich, to be exact. As I mulled over this passage, I realized that I am not a Proverbs 31 woman. My intention here is not to cut down *any* part of the Bible. If God breathed it, I believe it. But I have realized that this Proverbs 31 woman is the "ideal deal"—someone we can all hope to be and should strive to be. Some of us may have parts of her, but I doubt any of us have all of her attributes. Yep, I am more of an Isaiah 54 woman.

As I started to write this book, I decided to read every book I could find on the subject. I found excellent, scholarly commentaries (a wonderful friend who is all about research helped me by letting me borrow his books) about the prophet Isaiah and the Book he wrote. Of course, the prophet Isaiah was writing to the children of Israel. He was talking to a weary bunch who thought they had been forgotten in exile (hmmm,

I'm already seeing a parallel here…) by the Lord, as it says in Isaiah 40:27, *"Why do you say, O Jacob, and speak, O Israel: 'My way is hidden from the Lord, and my just claim is passed over by my God.'"* Yet Isaiah's message to them offered a different image of God as their deliverer. Even the great prophet Isaiah's own name reveals to Israel that the Lord saves; in Hebrew it is *Yesha'yahu,* which signifies the "Salvation of Jehovah."[1]

I gleaned words from these borrowed books, *The Interlinear Bible, The Holman Old Testament Commentary, The Pulpit Commentary,* and my own *Stone Edition of the Hebrew Tanach,* as well as many others. These studies told of the prophecies Isaiah had, and I came away with some awesome insight. After reading these books and commentaries, I would quiet my soul and listen to the Holy Spirit, seeking His commentary on these passages that Isaiah wrote through the Spirit all those years ago.

Isaiah 54 has always been such a personal read for me. I've lived it and made it my own. I encourage you to read it over and over and see what you can gain from it personally. This book is not only for the single person but also for those who have felt or been isolated, rejected, or lost. It speaks to both men and women, young and old, and even for the times and seasons of this day. As we dive into Isaiah 54, I believe the start of your victory is here too. Now, let's explore the precious jewels and gems of this great chapter! Thank You, Jesus!

ENDNOTE

1. *The Pulpit Commentary* (Grand Rapids, MI: Wm. B. Eerdmans Publishing Company, 1975), s.v. "Yesha'yahu."

Isaiah 54

¹"Sing, O barren, you who have not borne! Break forth into singing, and cry aloud, you who have not labored with child!

For more are the children of the desolate than the children of the married woman," says the Lord.

² "Enlarge the place of your tent, and let them stretch out the curtains of your dwellings; do not spare; lengthen your cords, and strengthen your stakes.

³For you shall expand to the right and to the left, and your descendants will inherit the nations, and make the desolate cities inhabited.

⁴"Do not fear, for you will not be ashamed; neither be disgraced, for you will not be put to shame; for you will forget the shame of your youth, and will not remember the reproach of your widowhood anymore.

⁵For your Maker is your husband, the Lord of hosts is His name; and your Redeemer is the Holy One of Israel; He is called the God of the whole earth.

⁶For the Lord has called you like a woman forsaken and grieved in spirit, like a youthful wife when you were refused," says your God.

⁷"For a mere moment I have forsaken you, but with great mercies I will gather you.

[8]*With a little wrath I hid My face from you for a moment; but with everlasting kindness I will have mercy on you," says the Lord, your Redeemer.*

[9]*"For this is like the waters of Noah to Me; for as I have sworn that the waters of Noah would no longer cover the earth, so have I sworn that I would not be angry with you, nor rebuke you.*

[10]*For the mountains shall depart and the hills be removed, but My kindness shall not depart from you, nor shall My covenant of peace be removed," says the Lord, who has mercy on you.*

[11]*"O you afflicted one, tossed with tempest, and not comforted, behold, I will lay your stones with colorful gems, and lay your foundations with sapphires.*

[12]*I will make your pinnacles of rubies, your gates of crystal, and all your walls of precious stones.*

[13]*All your children shall be taught by the Lord, and great shall be the peace of your children.*

[14]*In righteousness you shall be established; you shall be far from oppression, for you shall not fear; and from terror, for it shall not come near you.*

[15]*Indeed they shall surely assemble, but not because of Me. Whoever assembles against you shall fall for your sake.*

[16]*"Behold, I have created the blacksmith who blows the coals in the fire, who brings forth an instrument for his work; and I have created the spoiler to destroy.*

[17]*No weapon formed against you shall prosper, and every tongue which rises against you in judgment you shall condemn.*

This is the heritage of the servants of the Lord, and their righteousness is from Me," says the Lord.

Chapter One

GET READY TO PRAISE HIM!

"Sing, O barren, you who have not borne! Break forth into singing, and cry aloud, you who have not labored with child! For more are the children of the desolate than the children of the married woman," says the Lord (Isaiah 54:1).

Infertility. It is a devastating burden for some. Fortunately, I never had to deal with this personally, but of course, we all know many who have. My mother and father were some of the many. They were trying to have children back in the 1940s, a time when fertility tests were not even heard of. They just weren't able to have children. I remember my mom telling me, "They thought it was me, but they never knew for sure the reason why." She must have been devastated, although she never talked about it much. I guess somehow she learned to trust in the Lord and accept this fate. My dad also mentioned to me that he expected to have a houseful of children. Dad also was perplexed by the fact that he and mom were established, well-to-do farmers in the area yet childless, while people as poor as church mice were able to have many children.

Who understands the ways of God? His ways are higher, and His thoughts are higher (see Isa. 55:8-9). If my parents had been able to have children, I do not know if I would have gotten to meet the most wonderful set of parents anyone could ever have. Almost 20 years after they were married, they adopted my brother and me. We were not biologically brother and sister. They adopted my brother at about 2 years of age, and I came along about three years later.

I was 3 days old when they went down to St. Petersburg, Florida, to pick up their little bundle of joy. God is so sovereign, at work at all times, especially when we need Him most. My mom and dad always told me that I was special because of being adopted—that I was chosen, and they made me feel that way. I found out many years later that I was the product of an unmarried couple. I was conceived in Germany, born in Florida, and raised in Northern Illinois. The amazing part is that these plans were put in motion when my father and mother weren't able to conceive, and then Father God Himself placed cousins of my mom and dad in the St. Petersburg area.

Jim was a cousin of my dad, and his wife Beverly was having a baby at the same time that my biological mother was, and they both happened to be going to the same doctor. Bev was quite a woman, someone I always admired. She ran her own realty company in St. Pete, and her husband, Jim, managed the local municipal airport.

The doctor happened to mention to Bev, "Do you know of a couple looking for a child? I have an unwed mother who is coming in here who needs to give her baby up for adoption." In the '60s, that's what happened if you were unmarried and having a baby—you gave the child up for adoption. Bev replied, "I have just the couple who needs a child." That set in motion the adoption process for me and my parents to meet. I have always been thankful to Bev and Jim for that.

Perhaps you are one who has wrestled with the pain of infertility. Who knows what plans the Lord has in store for you and a child somewhere who needs a home? Remember Isaiah 55:8, *"For My thoughts are not your thoughts, nor are your ways My ways,' says the Lord."*

ADOPTION

I know of a very committed couple who have had this same devastating news regarding not being able to have a child. Wouldn't you know, at the time of this writing (and the soon-to-be father has just hit 40), the good Lord has put into motion an adoption for their new son, Caleb, who is 10 years old. What an amazing God story! This couple even named their children before they were married: *Caleb* if it's a boy and *Abigail* if it's a girl. So when the adoption agency called with the news of a son to adopt, this couple was elated to discover that the boy's name was Caleb. They haven't renamed him. That already *was* his name. Wow!

Of course, not everyone's experience ends so joyfully. One of my best friends conceived twice and both times birthed a beautiful baby boy. They were born less than two years apart. Both died almost at birth. They lived on life support till the doctors could figure out what was wrong. In layman's terms, it was some type of misconnection between the muscles and nerves. They had to pull the life support, as the boys would have always had to be on it. And of course, they would not have made it much longer since these sons had no movement. These were beautifully formed, *healthy-looking* baby boys, but internally they could not survive.

I remember telling my friend, as I visited her in a faraway children's hospital, "This is every parent's worst nightmare." Yet, this couple courageously picked themselves up and adopted two foster boys, brothers out of an abusive home. The road hasn't been easy for any of them. The oldest boy has landed in prison. It seems he isn't breaking out of the inner prison that is holding him. My friend, who has somehow found peace in all this, says she doesn't know if her oldest son "will ever find peace." But I know the Healer, the One who can do it.

Even in the darkest and most desperate situations, we must keep praying for that one Word from Heaven. One Word from the Lord Himself will break our loved ones out of their prisons and will heal our broken ones' inner wounds. That one Word from the Lord is for *our* breakthrough too.

At times, Father has used others to bring that word to me, or He has used me to bring an encouraging word to others. *"The Lord God has given Me the tongue of the learned, that I should know how to speak a word in season to him who is weary..."* (Isa. 50:4). In Greek, it is called a *rhema* word, a word in due season. It is a word that speaks to your heart, and you know that it's just for you at that moment.

Thinking of mine and my friend's stories, I am reminded of the beauty of adoption. What a wonderful parallel of what our Father has done for us. Romans 8:15-17 declares:

> *For you did not receive the spirit of bondage again to fear, but you received the Spirit of adoption by whom we cry out, "Abba, Father." The Spirit Himself bears witness with our spirit that we are children of God, and if children, then heirs—heirs of God and joint heirs with Christ...*

When we are adopted into families, we become "joint heirs" with our brothers and sisters (even if they're not biological) in that family. In God's family, *we* are one in Yeshua (Jesus's Hebrew name), one in the olive tree because we are grafted in (see Rom. 11:18-24). God has not left us or forsaken us; He has placed us right smack dab in the middle of His family where we are all joint heirs with Christ Himself! Wow!

I like what my rabbi (whom I'll be formally introducing in a later chapter) had to say about adoptions and step-children. He said that in Jewish families, once a person is adopted or marries into a family, there is no "this is my step-child," "this is my adopted child," or even "this is my step-sister." It's "this is my child or sister or brother." That person is considered chosen, and that is that.

Thinking back on my own family (we were not Jewish that I know of), I always remember that's how my parents treated me—like I had been chosen...a special child. I may have had cousins who didn't think that way at the time, but you wouldn't have wanted to tell that to my dad or mom! Come to think of it, you may not want to tell that to my Daddy God either!

RESTORATION COMING

So dear ones, those who have felt like a "barren woman," here is God's promise to you:

Enlarge the place of your tent, and let them stretch out the curtains of your dwellings; do not spare; lengthen your cords, and strengthen your stakes (Isaiah 54:2).

I have been blessed to participate with an intercessory prayer team called Prepare the Way Ministries that travels all across this great nation of ours and prays over the land, waterways, towns, cities, and so forth. I have met this group when they came into town or local area. One thing that stands out in particular is the actual act of driving stakes (like tent pegs) into the ground. Verse 2 of Isaiah 54 says, *"Do not spare...strengthen your stakes."* It's just a physical act as we pray for forgiveness over the land for things that we, or even our forefathers, have done. As we pray for forgiveness, we then pray for our Father God's righteousness and healing over the land. James Nesbit, the leader of the prayer team, describes it as "staking our claim for the Lord" and "putting our own DNA in the ground."[1]

I studied for months (with nothing forthcoming) over these particular verses in Isaiah, trying to get revelation and knowledge about what Father would have me to say about them. Then I happened to attend a worship service at an International House of Prayer in Springfield, Illinois. As we entered into quiet worship with the music low, just waiting on the Lord, the leader of the service started to say, "Enlarge your tent pegs, lengthen them out, allow Father to come in and strengthen you; let Him go where no one ever has." Amen!

Months later, I found a trinket in Zechariah 10:3-6:

...For the Lord of hosts will visit His flock, the house of Judah [which means "praise"].... From him comes the cornerstone, from him the tent peg...I will strengthen the house of Judah....

In this passage, the Lord of hosts—Jehovah Sabaoth—is getting ready to restore Israel. Of course, there's a battle first when God is getting ready to restore you. (Could the battle be in *the waiting* itself?) When you start reading and hearing continually about tent pegs or stakes (and it resonates in your soul), get ready! Restoration is near, and I don't know about you, but I'm ready to be restored and rebuilt by the Lord Himself!

WAITING ON THE PROMISE

In light of this, Isaiah 40:31 comes to mind:

But those who wait on the Lord shall renew their strength; they shall mount up with wings like eagles, they shall run and not be weary, they shall walk and not faint.

Years ago, while I was going through my divorce, a friend of mine gave me a card with an eagle flying in a forest. I have always thought of the above verse when looking at that card. As you wait in your trials, dear hearts, let our precious Lord renew your strength like the eagles. Let Him strengthen your stakes; let Him expand you to the right and to the left. There's hope in your trial; there's hope at the end of your tunnel. You may not see it now, but there is!

Strong's Exhaustive Concordance lists *wait* (*chakah* in Hebrew) as "to adhere to, long, tarry, wait."[2] The tarry part often seems longer than we'd like it to be for those of us *"who are perishing"* (see Deut. 4:26). However, I like the way the commentary in my Bible describes *wait*, "In Scripture, the word 'wait' normally suggests the anxious, yet confident, expectation by God's people that the Lord will intervene on their behalf." Let this last part wash over you... "Waiting, therefore, is the working out of hope."[3]

Diving further into Isaiah 40, it seems Father is saying, "Hey, take notice here! Quit looking to others and other things!" Look at Isaiah 40:21-22:

Have you not known? Have you not heard? ...It is He who sits above the circle of the earth...who stretches out the heavens like a curtain, and spreads them out like a tent to dwell in.

I can envision Abba Father as He sits on His throne looking down and asking a couple of His mighty angels to pull back the curtains. He wants to see what is going on down here. He wants to know: "Hello, hey you down there...who is calling on Me for My help?"

For you shall expand to the right and to the left, and your descen-dants will inherit the nations, and make the desolate cities inhabited (Isaiah 54:3).

Just as Isaiah was encouraging Israel to get ready, to expand those tent pegs to the right and to the left for their many children, so the Lord encourages you. He sounds like a husband encouraging his wife, particularly if the house is empty. Maybe the house—your house—is desolate for the moment; now Father is saying, "There's more to come; look up here!"

I know my house seems desolate. Oh, it may not be just children we're waiting for. Maybe we're waiting on a healing or our help-meet or for our "ship to come in." Waiting involves trust. Waiting surely involves a test. As we wait, we want assurance that He will fill up our emptiness in His perfect timing. I believe that all He asks now is for us to wait in obedience. One of my favorite songs in the movie *Fireproof* says:

> I'm waiting
>
> I'm waiting on you, Lord
>
> And I am hopeful
>
> I'm waiting on you, Lord
>
> Though it is painful
>
> But patiently I will wait
>
> I will move ahead, bold and confident
>
> Taking every step in obedience...[4]

This is not a "works" message, as Ephesians 2:9 says it's *"not of works, lest anyone should boast."* Instead, it is a *"love and relationship"* message. My Bible has bold red letters (which signifies Yeshua talking). He said, *"If you love Me, keep My commandments"* (John 14:15). May we all get so snuggled up to the Father, Son, and Holy Spirit in love that struggling with *whatever* is no longer an issue!

TWO TYPES OF OBEDIENCE

We've traveled from waiting to obedience, which really puts us in a test. I'm in one at the moment. Some of my tests I've been dealing with for years. In all my reading, I have found two different kinds of obedience. Look at what is often called the "obedience chapter," Deuteronomy 28:

> *Now it shall come to pass, if you diligently obey the voice of the Lord your God, to observe carefully all His commandments...all these blessings shall come upon you and overtake you, because you obey the voice of the Lord your God* (Deuteronomy 28:1-2).

First are the blessings that come from obeying the voice of the Lord. As my pastor puts it, "Blessings come into our lives when we do what God tells us to do." Oh, we'll suffer at times, still have our battles, but blessings will come. The Book of Second Kings is full of examples. The Lord spoke, and as people obeyed, they got their blessings. Jehoshaphat, king of Judah, looked for a prophet to inquire about the mess he and Jehoram, king of Israel, were about to get into. They were going to war but without water for their armies or their animals.

As they spoke to Elisha the prophet, Elisha called for a musician (praise before a battle!) and then the *"hand of the Lord came upon him"* (2 Kings 3:15). Elisha told them to dig ditches, which was not a small feat before the days of tractors and backhoes. However, when they obeyed, the Lord filled them with water after the morning offering. Poof! Instant watering hole; they got strength from *their* God—*their* Defender—for the battle at hand. They obeyed, and Father God provided.

In Second Kings 4, the prophet Elisha is called upon by a poor widow woman whose sons are about to be taken as payment for credit that's due. Think about that for a moment. She's about to lose her sons as slaves! Elisha wants to know what she has in the house, and she tells him *"nothing... but a jar of oil"* (2 Kings 4:2). He tells her to borrow many jars—empty vessels—and when she's gathered them, to shut the door behind her and her sons. As she starts to pour the little bit of oil from the jar, it multiplies until she has no more vessels left to fill! Elisha tells her to sell the oil to pay her debt off; then she and her sons can live on the rest. This widow woman and her sons obeyed, and Father God provided.

This was not just true in Elisha's day, but it applies to us as well. *"Today, if you will hear His voice, do not harden your hearts as in the rebellion"* (Heb. 3:15). Sometimes I wonder if the reason we don't see miracles like Elisha and the people did is because we are the ones not heeding His voice. Perhaps we are the ones not moving in His direction.

Despair should not be the only reason we draw near to Him. Our Father loves it when we lavish our praise on Him, when we praise, worship, and adore Him. In later chapters, I will share testimonies of walking out praise and obedience. My pastor just preached a message about this very subject and emphasized that "God blesses obedience, and obedience opens up the miracle-working power of God!" I say "Amen!" to Pastor Don on that one!

Second is obedience to the written Word—*"to observe carefully all His commandments"* (Deut. 28:1). The Ten Commandments are a really good place to start (see Exod. 20:1-17). I like what Yeshua said to the Pharisees when they asked which was the greatest commandment. He said:

> *"You shall love the Lord your God with all your heart, with all your soul, and with all your mind." This is the first and great commandment. And the second is like it: "You shall love your neighbor as yourself"* (Matthew 22:37-39).

Have you ever noticed in Deuteronomy 28 that the curses seem to outweigh the blessings by about four to one? Here's the key. The Father likes it when we offer Him praise and sacrifice. The Word says in First Samuel 15:22, *"Has the Lord as great delight in burnt offerings and sacrifices, as in obeying the voice of the Lord?..."* He loves it when we sacrifice to Him. He delights in it! The verse continues, *"...to obey is better than sacrifice...."* Verse 23 says, *"For rebellion is as the sin of witchcraft...."* There's that word *rebellion* again. *Whoa!* Better to stay in obedience, dear ones.

For the single person especially, loneliness can take hold, and many start getting into trouble. It is painful. I know; I've been single for over 15 years since my divorce. Waiting for things we believe are coming to pass is difficult; there is suffering. Don't let anyone kid you. Don't you just love it when people who don't even have a clue about what you're going through try to give you advice? They have no idea! They don't know how tough it is paying the bills by yourself, how hard it is having no one to bounce ideas off of or to cover your back, so to speak.

Of course, some of the loneliest people in the world are married. I was one of them and speak from experience. It's better to suffer while in obedience rather than in sin. Getting out of fellowship with our Father God will only compound the problem.

TRUST—THE FINAL PIECE

We've traveled from waiting to obedience. We have just one more element to add to our sequence: *trust*. Are we going to trust Him? Really *trust Him?* Then we must cry out to Him, declaring our pain. "But Father, I am lonely...I am hurting...Father, don't You see my hurt, my tears? Do You not understand, Lord?" He is a safe place for sharing our hurts and fears.

The Bible holds many nuggets for us about the word *trust*. One of my favorite Scriptures to lean on is Proverbs 3:5-6:

> *Trust in the Lord with all your heart, and lean not on your own understanding; in all your ways acknowledge Him, and He shall direct your paths.*

We may not understand it all, but when we trust and lean on Him, He will show us the way through our pain.

As I write this, I'm just coming off a very difficult holiday season—a very difficult year all-around. I feel the pain of having an estranged precious daughter; we both let the enemy come in and steal our relationship. I lost commercial cleaning jobs due to the economy. As so many have, I also lost money in the market. I was even engaged to be married, but that didn't work out either. The break-up was on mutual terms, so it ended well for both of us.

I got so low that I even let the enemy come in to the point that I thought of ending it. "No more pain...no more suffering," satan would say. I realized he was quoting the Word of God at me, but in a twisted way. That's what satan did to Yeshua during His 40 days in the wilderness too (see Matt. 4:1-11). However, I chose to listen to the voice of God—"There is hope! Put your trust in Me. Let me bear your burdens. I, Yeshua, have taken your pain; I have taken your suffering!"

I love First Peter 4:12-13:

> *Beloved, do not think it strange concerning the fiery trial which is to try you, as though some strange thing happened to you; but rejoice to the extent that you partake of Christ's sufferings, that when His glory is revealed, you may also be glad with exceeding joy.*

When the Word puts everything in perspective, God's joy will flood our souls again. Praise God!

At times, however, the enemy likes to wake me early in the morning, and from the first moments, the fight is on. Sound familiar? I wallow till I get to the lowest point, when it all looks hopeless (remember, the enemy is doing this), but somehow I force myself to get up, put on some praise music, and praise! I call it "Judah Praise!" Judah's name means "Let God be Praised." Genesis 29:35 says (Leah speaking), *"Now I will praise the Lord.' Therefore she called his name Judah...."*

Praise in the Battle

Start to praise Him, dear ones, for you are in the midst of a battle, and Judah goes first in battle. You have to praise Him first! In the first chapter of the Book of Judges, all of Israel was in a continuing military conquest against their enemies.

The children of Israel asked the Lord "Who shall be first to go up for us against the Canaanites to fight against them?" And the Lord said "Judah shall go up. Indeed I have delivered the land into his hand" (Judges 1:1-2).

Who isn't in a war, a battle, especially in these endtimes? The world, it seems, has forgotten the Lord. We and our children are pulled in every direction as we trudge daily through this life. Then add to everything else the images from television, billboards, magazines, and the like. Some of us do everything we can to blot it out, but it still is overwhelming at times, isn't it? However, when we start to praise Him, our praise opens the portals of Heaven and starts to change the atmosphere, not only in the heavenlies but also here on earth.

When I praise Him, it gets my mind off of the fear, hopelessness, and despair the enemy wants to keep me mired in, and it puts it back where it should be—meditating on our Father God, our Maker, our Husband, our Provider, Healer, and Deliverer. Praise God!

Look at this. The very first verse of Isaiah 54 says, *"Sing...break forth into singing...."* The Hebrew Tanach puts it this way: *"Sing out, O barren one who has not given birth; break into glad song and be jubilant!"* I thought I had finished with verse 1, but the Holy Spirit called me back to it, saying, "Look again...we are to sing...be jubilant!" This chapter starts with praise!

I can't talk about praise without recognizing Abba Father for who He is. I quoted Romans 8:15-17 earlier, but let's look at it again: *"You received the Spirit of adoption by whom we cry out, 'Abba, Father.'"* When I looked *abba* up in the commentary of my Bible, it almost brought me to tears. It says, "Abba was what a little Hebrew child would call his father."[5] It's a close, intimate, personal term of endearment. Yeshua would have used *abba* to call on His father Joseph while He lived here on earth.

You may have noticed that I like to call Jesus by His Hebrew name, Yeshua (it means salvation). Yeshua is what Mary, His dear mother, would have called Him. Isn't it neat to think of it that way? It's kind of like calling our Father, Abba Father, our Daddy God. Yes, the Father, Son, and Holy Spirit want that much intimacy with us—how blessed and humbled and highly favored we are!

Yeshua also used *Abba* when He was crying out in the Garden of Gethsemane right before He was taken to be crucified by the Roman soldiers (see Mark 14:36). None of the disciples could stay awake even for one hour. Yeshua knew that only His alone time with His Abba Father could give Him the strength He needed for what lay ahead.

How about you? There will come a time when you will have to go to the Garden of Gethsemane. Most times this is the result of soul-wrenching anguish, unbearable trials, and racking pain. No one person, no one thing will be able to give you the answer you need. It's one-on-one time with your personal God and Savior. Cry out to your Abba Father in your trial, precious ones, because when you do, He will give you the strength to get through it!

THE NAMES OF GOD

A few months ago, I had the privilege of going with friends to a Benny Hinn conference in Louisville, Kentucky. One of those precious friends picked up a book for me that Pastor Hinn wrote called *The Names of God.* When we recognize the names of Father God—*Adonai,* our Lord and Master; *El Shaddai,* the All-Sufficient One; *Elohim,* our Creator; *Jehovah-Rapha,* the Lord that Healeth; and *Jehovah-Shalom,* the Lord is Peace—they lead us into praise. Speaking those names with the reverence and awe God deserves puts us into highest praise. We must find that rest, that peace of *Jehovah-Shalom.* We must find joy in His provision as *Jehovah-Jireh.* As Pastor Benny wrote in his book, "Let the names of God transform your faith!"[6]

It doesn't stop there. Because of our broken relationship with Him due to the fall of Adam, Father God sent His precious Son Yeshua to die on that cross for us. Yeshua even took stripes (a beating) for our peace! That just amazes me! Isaiah 53:5 says:

> *He was wounded for our transgressions, He was bruised for our iniquities, the chastisement of our peace [Shalom] was upon Him, and by His stripes, we are healed [Jehovah-Rapha].*

Yeshua took the mystery of those 39 lashes of a whip for us! I have heard it said that medical science has found 39 root causes for *all* diseases! When I heard that information, I started shaking and thinking, *Wow!* So don't tell me that healing isn't for today. As I will share in a later chapter, I am living proof that Yeshua still heals.

Salvation is the most important gift in anyone's life. Yeshua, the one true living God, gives it freely if we will only believe and accept Him into our hearts. Then, as we learn of Abba Father through His Word and through His Holy Spirit, He lovingly draws us closer and closer into relationship with Him. In our love walk with Him, *even when trouble comes* (even if it's of our own doing!), He does not leave us. As a matter of fact, His Word tells us what to do (praise, obedience, sacrifice). I can hear Him calling, "Praise Me, dear ones. Walk in obedience to Me, My love. I will take care of you."

PRAYER NUGGET:

Most gracious and heavenly Father, Baruch Atah Adonai, blessed are You, O Lord our God, for You are El Roi, the God Who Sees, and You have shown us all things and put all things before us and under our feet. Your Word goes before us to strengthen us, uphold us, deliver us. You are right there upholding us with Your righteous right hand. You deliver us right where we are, for You O Lord have promised, "And those who know Thy name will put their trust in Thee; for Thou, O Lord, hast not forsaken those who seek Thee" (Ps. 9:10 KJV). Help us seek You, Lord, like never before. We need a higher revelation of You, Father God, and You have promised that those who seek You will find You. So, enlarge our hearts, stretch out our tent pegs. As we go forth in praise and obedi-ence, help us, Holy Spirit, to look only to You and Your promises as we study this great Word given to us through Isaiah. Praise You, Father! We ask it all in the mighty name of Yeshua, Christ Jesus. Amen.

ENDNOTES

1.   James Nesbit (interview); http://www.ptwministries.com.

2.   James Strong, *Strong's Exhaustive Concordance* (Peabody, MA: Henrickson Publishers), Hebrew #2442.

3.   *Nelson NKJV Study Bible* (Nashville, TN: Thomas Nelson), commentary on Isaiah 40:31.

4.   John Waller, "While I'm Waiting," lyrics at http://www.stlyrics.com/lyrics/fireproof/whileimwaiting.htm; accessed August 3, 2011.

5.   *Nelson NKJV Study Bible*, commentary on Romans 8:15-17.

6.   Benny Hinn, *The Names of God* (Dallas, TX: Bookmark Publishing, 2008).

PERSONAL
Notes

_____

_____

_____

_____

_____

_____

_____

_____

_____

_____

_____

_____

_____

_____

_____

_____

_____

_____

_____

_____

_____

_____

Chapter Two

MAGNIFY HIM—NOT
OUR FEAR!

Do not fear, for you will not be ashamed; neither be disgraced,
for you will not be put to shame; for you will forget the shame of
your youth, and will not remember the reproach of your widow-
hood anymore (Isaiah 54:4).

Let's talk about fear for a moment. There have been, no doubt, volumes written on this subject. Fear debilitates us, paralyzes us, and renders us useless; it can put a grip on us like no other. But what does the Word say about fear? I like the way the King James Version says, *"For the enemy hath magnified himself"* (Lam. 1:9). Have you ever thought and thought and continue to think of things that really (if you thought about it), will most likely never, ever happen? I have. I go off on these tangents of thought that are really nothing more than fear—and it seems I'm letting the enemy "magnify himself." *"Fear the Lord, and depart from evil,"* as His Word tells us to do (Prov. 3:7). Think of this as a holy and reverent fear of our Father, a humble respect and submission. Matthew 10:28 tells us:

> *And do not fear those who kill the body but cannot kill the soul.*
> *But rather fear Him who is able to destroy both soul and body*
> *in hell.*

Wow!

The truth is, fear grips all of us at one time or another. Sometimes it is good, like when we get that gut feeling that tells us to turn back or go another way when we sense that something is not quite right. However, there are times when we have unhealthy fears—fears that hold us back from trying something new, something unknown. The enemy might be saying here, "Oh don't do that; you're not smart enough, you're too old, too used, too *whatever....*"

A few years ago, I took a friend of mine (who had been recently diagnosed with multiple sclerosis) to St. Louis to a place called Joan Gieson's Ministry of Love. I had just heard Joan speaking on a local Christian television station about her testimony of healing from multiple sclerosis at a Kathryn Kuhlman meeting. Just a day or two after I heard Joan's testimony, my friend called me and told me her diagnosis. I told her about what I had just heard, and we made plans to go to Joan's ministry within the week.

My friend was not the only one who needed healing. I too had had some recent health issues creeping back into my life, issues that I had previously been healed of (as I will share in more detail in Chapter 5). We are in a daily battle, dear hearts. The enemy was trying to steal my healing, but I was determined to resist.

> *Be sober, be vigilant: because your adversary the devil walks about like a roaring lion, seeking whom he may devour. Resist him, steadfast in the faith...* (1 Peter 5:8-9).

My friend and I were both ministered to by the wonderful saints at the Ministry of Love. I remember specifically a prophetic word given to me by one of the dear sisters. She said the enemy was attacking my mind (especially with fear) more than anything. I knew she had "hit the nail on the head." She highly recommended a book called *Battlefield of the Mind* by Joyce Meyer.[1] I encourage anyone who is battling *anything* to read this book. It sheds light on who the real enemy is and what he tries to get a hold of: our minds.

One of my favorite verses about fear, one I've been able to use to help others, is a verse that the Holy Spirit gave me as I spoke with another woman. I was living temporarily in Tennessee at the time, staying with my mother, who had fallen and broken her hip. This was a very hard time in my life. I had just been date-raped for the second time in less than four months. I had gone to my pastor (who was a woman), and she wisely advised me to get counseling. I remember sitting at a group counseling session, and after our leader had her session with us, we were then encouraged to talk among ourselves.

I started talking with a woman who was about my age and began sharing Scriptures with her. As I recall, I gave her a couple of passages that really weren't resonating with her or grabbing her soul yet. Finally, as I was thumbing through the Word, I came to a verse and blurted out: *"For God has not given us a spirit of fear, but of power and of love and of a sound mind"* (2 Tim. 1:7).

All of a sudden, a look of shock enveloped her as her eyes started to tear up, and she said, "How did you know? How did you know! There is a history of mental illness in my family, and I have been in fear that it would be me next, yet you just told me I could have a sound mind!" She started to cry and told me she felt she would be able to go on with her life now. I looked over at our counselor, who had been listening to all this.

She said, "I don't know what you have, but whatever it is, don't lose it." Wow! That Word, that wonderful, living Word from our Lord *"...is living and powerful, and sharper than any two-edged sword..."* (Heb. 4:12).

GOING DEEPER

I need to preface the following paragraphs with a "word of warning." This is going to go deeper than many of us would like to go. I don't know why it is, but it seems that to get rid of a trauma in our lives, we have to bring it up and experience the depth of that affliction in order to heal from it. Jehovah-Rapha, our Healer, our Great Physician already has the prescription in hand. A paraphrase of James 5:16 comes to mind—*confess and be healed; confess and be healed!* I've experienced this several times in my own life and have found it especially true for pains that have been buried way down deep. There's an old adage, "Things that are covered don't heal well."

Keep in mind that Abba Father wants to heal you from these deep wounds and trauma to your soul. Expose it all to the light of Yeshua. Hebrews 13:8 says, *"Jesus Christ is the same yesterday, today and forever."* He doesn't change, dear hearts. He can heal and wants to heal your past hurts. When I start dreaming a lot about the past, I know He's trying to show me something that He and I *both* need to deal with. Healing is here! Pass through those deep waters, dear hearts, to get to the other side!

If you don't believe in evil spirits attaching to and following people around, listen to this! One day, as I was trying to make sense of it all (after my second date-rape), a voice came out of nowhere and said in my mind, "You ought to be dating women; at least they can't rape you." I thought, *Where did that come from?* I spoke about it to a spiritual mentor, and she told me to "just be careful."

About a week after this "voice" spoke to me, I went to my chiropractor, who was a woman. During my session, she grabbed my hand, pulling it toward her in a way that made me feel uncomfortable. I immediately pulled it back, and as I left, I began to think of all the things she had said to me during my last few visits with her. Again, I went back to my spiritual friend to tell her what had happened. She said, "Oh, she's coming on to you."

I said, "Nooo! I'm not like that."

She countered, "I know, but be careful..."

After that, I could see that not only had satan been whispering stuff in my ear, but he had also provided someone to entice me and try to get me involved in a lesbian relationship!

I really had some struggles at that point, and I had just about had it with men in my life. By the grace of God—through my own prayers, the prayers of others, and my knowledge of the Scriptures—I was able to withstand the enemy's plot. One of the passages that held me fast was First Corinthians 6:9-10:

> *Do you not know that the unrighteous will not inherit the kingdom of God? Do not be deceived. Neither fornicators, nor idolaters, nor adulterers, nor homosexuals, nor sodomites, nor thieves, nor covetous, nor drunkards, nor revilers, nor extortioners will inherit the kingdom of God.*

I chose not to take that path, just as I believe one can choose to be faithful in a marriage (not commit adultery) or choose not to steal or lie. I know how easy it is to get caught in sin; and I know how passionately God loves the adulterer, the drunkard, and the homosexual. Yet He asks us not to act in sin—*"do not be deceived,"* as the Bible declares (Gal. 6:7)! So if you have fallen into sin, stop it! You will inherit His holy Kingdom if you do.

Ministering to other wounded souls has helped me to deal with life's obstacles. Please, dear ones, don't be afraid to talk to others about a trauma in your life. There is truly nothing better than being able to have someone who can share good, godly wisdom and counsel. One of my favorite sayings is, "You have to get real before you can heal!" When you have gone through difficulties and you allow the Holy Spirit to work through you to help others in the same situation, it will transform your life!

Not Flesh and Blood

Unfortunately, a couple of years later, I experienced a third date-rape. As I reached out to Father, the Holy Spirit gave me a powerful Scripture (see Isa. 51), and through it the evil spirit connected with those rapes was broken from my life.

I had just moved back to Illinois and was hoping for a new life, hoping to put the old behind me. I had been here almost two years when I started seeing someone (we met through mutual friends). I won't go into the details, but I had been seeing this man for over two months and had started to put some trust in him. However, on one of those dates, he took me by force in what I perceived to be one of the most violent crimes against me ever. I could see the hate flowing from him. I remember coming home and just being numb. The enemy was saying to me, "You caused this; it's your fault. If you hadn't had done this, if you hadn't done that..." on and on and on.

(I will insert a word of caution here to those who may be reading this and judging the situation. Rebuke that judgmental spirit and ask for forgiveness if you've been judging others. With that spirit, you will not be able to help others or get the help you yourself may need.)

I went to church that Sunday but wasn't even able to stay in the sanctuary. I went into a room that was empty and just cried and poured my heart out to God asking, "Why, God, why?" And then I opened the Word right to Isaiah 51:

> Listen to Me, you who follow after righteousness, you who seek the Lord.... For the Lord will comfort Zion [me], He will comfort all her waste places... (Isaiah 51:1,3).

I knew right then and there that this verse was for me. As I read to the end of the chapter, I knew I had been released from this terrible spirit, for the Word said:

> But I will put it into the hand of those who afflict you, who have said to you, "Lie down, that we may walk over you." And you have laid your body like the ground, and as the street, for those who walk over (Isaiah 51:23).

Here it was, my very own *rhema* word! Praise God! That was well over 10 years ago, and I haven't had that evil spirit come around me since! Claim this for yourself, dear ones!

NO FEAR IN LOVE

Recently the Lord showed me a situation in which a spirit of fear seemed to be wrapping its tentacles around some dear brothers and sisters in the Lord. They were part of a Christian motorcycle group. A woman had recently joined them, and a lot of people knew her past history (which delved into witchcraft and prostitution), and some were "afraid of her," to use a phrase from one of the leaders there. I was eating supper together with this group and heard them discussing it.

I leaned over and said, "This is really none of my business, but if you would like to hear what I have to say about this, I will tell you." They encouraged me to go on as I prayed quickly and quietly in the Holy Spirit for the right words to say. I started with, "I don't know about you all, but I welcome this type of situation to see where my walk with the Lord is. If I'm scared of it, then it means I'm not focusing right. Don't focus on her past, on her bits of disruption, or any of that."

I was really searching for words at this point, and I just felt the word *love* come out. So I said, "Just *love* her." Then I added, "Remember, greater is *He* (Jesus) who is in you, than he who is in the world." (See First John 4:4.)

Many in the group agreed and said they felt it was confirmation, as they too had felt they should just love her. As I was pondering this, another Scripture came to mind: *"There is no fear in love; but perfect love casts out fear, because fear involves torment. But he who fears has not been made perfect in love"* (1 John 4:18).

Remember I said earlier that I welcome this type of situation? If we fear, we are not being made perfect in love. There is a check in our spirit-man for us. Of course, there are Scriptures about deliverance and binding evil forces: *"Whatever you bind on earth will be bound in heaven..."* (Matt. 18:18). Also, there are excellent studies written on the subject of deliverance, but this goes beyond the scope of what I feel Father wants me to say here at this particular time. Christ's blood has covered it all, dear ones. Remember, we must choose love.

A Sound Mind

A few years ago, I purchased a book called *Sparkling Gems From the Greek*. As I was writing this chapter, I picked that book up again, discovering a powerful insight into a Scripture I referenced earlier—Second Timothy 1:7: *"For God has not given us a spirit of fear, but of power and of love and of a sound mind."* I believe God really wants to highlight the truths in this verse.

Read author Rick Renner's Greek word study on this particular verse:

> I want to especially point your focus to the words "sound mind." This phrase is taken from the Greek word *sophroneo*, which is a compound word combining *sodzo* and *phroneo*. The Greek word *sodzo* means to be *saved* or *delivered*. It suggests something that is *delivered, rescued, revived, salvaged and protected* is now *safe* and *secure*. The second part of the phrase "sound mind" comes from the Greek word *phroneo* which carries the idea of a person's *intelligence or total frame of thinking*—including his *rationale, logic, and emotions.*

He goes on to say (and I love this!):

> The word *sophroneo* in Second Timothy 1:7 could be translated: "God has not given you a spirit of fear, but of power and of love—He has given you a mind that has been delivered, rescued, revived, salvaged, protected, and brought into a place of safety and security so that it is no longer affected by illogical, unfounded, and absurd thoughts."[2]

Why is it important to understand this? Because when you are beginning to live a life of faith—when you reach out to do the seemingly impossible—the enemy will try to assault you mentally, emotionally, spiritually, and even physically in an attempt to stop your progress. For instance, he may speak to our minds, saying things like, "You can't do this! This doesn't make any sense! Are you crazy?" When this happens, we must quote the Scripture at ol' beelzebub. For example, "You know I can do this because it says in Philippians 4:13 that I *can* do all things through Christ who strengthens me." Or, "I'm not crazy; I have a sound mind." Or even, "I have the mind of Christ!" (See First Corinthians 2:16.)

Yeshua gave us a perfect example of this when, early in His ministry, He went out to the desert to pray for 40 days. When the tempter came (and he will come), did our precious Lord and Savior get scared? Did He run the other way? No. He just quoted His Father's Word—that living, breathing, active Word back at the father of lies (see Luke 4:1-13). Amen! And we are to do it too if we want to live a victorious life in Yeshua.

THE SHAME OF OUR YOUTH

Isaiah 54:4 talks about *"the shame of your youth."* Ouch! Do we really want to go there? How many of us, as we look back over the years (or even look at our lives right now!) have more than a few things we are ashamed about? Yet Isaiah tells us, speaking for God, *"Neither be disgraced or ashamed...you will forget the shame of your youth."* Satan will try to make us feel guilty and ashamed, but Abba Father, through the precious blood of the Lamb, has forgiven those of us who believe in Him! Like a husband who forgives his wayward wife or a wife who forgives her straying husband, so Abba God has forgiven us.

When we hear voices of guilt or condemnation, which always come from satan, we must make sure that we recognize their source.

> *There is therefore now no condemnation to those who are in Christ Jesus, who do not walk according to the flesh, but according to the Spirit* (Romans 8:1).

However, at times we do feel a check in our spirits, a check that lets us know that the Father wants us to come into obedience to His will. That is called *conviction*. We must not confuse conviction, which is from the Holy Spirit, with condemnation, which is from the enemy. One important clue is confusion; if we feel confused about something, it is also from the enemy. *"For God is not the author of confusion, but of peace..."* (1 Cor. 14:33).

But if you are coming under conviction by the precious Holy Spirit, just comply with His will! It will be much easier than to keep on running or keep on sinning (or whatever it is) in disobedience to Him. Father God always knows what's best, and it's always for our good.

THE REPROACH OF WIDOWHOOD

Isaiah goes on, "[You] *will not remember the reproach of your widow-hood anymore"* (Isa. 54:4). I have never had to deal with widowhood, but I know many who have. I have a friend (she wrote the poem at the end of this book) who was widowed while she was only in her early 40s. I listen as she voices her heartache and loneliness yet see her faithfulness to the One above and, more importantly, His faithfulness to us as we cry out to Him.

I also think of all the sweet older ladies who sit in our church pews. My mother was one of them. I'm not sure what the statistics are, but it seems that for every ten widow ladies, there is only one widower. It amazes me as I look at these wise, grand ladies of beautiful strength and dignity. In the last couple of months alone, I know two wonderful women who have been left to go it alone. They are still faithful in coming to church, and I see a peace and serenity in them as they stay active in their faith, in their church, and in their callings.

I recall one pastor telling me about a lady in his church. This pastor told me that this woman and her husband were "sweethearts" throughout their marriage. However, her husband died in his early 60s. Yet the pastor said that she didn't shed a tear. She was so "rest-assured" that her husband was with the Lord and out of suffering here on this earth that she was a great and willing testimony to others of that hope and peace through Christ.

I encourage those who have been widowed, divorced, or even recently single for whatever reason to take this time to bring Father God into their lives as their Husband, the Lover of their souls. As the prophet goes on to say, *"For your Maker is your husband..."* (Isa. 54:5). Really, this includes all of us. Many married people are experiencing their own tests and trials and need the assurance of God's presence and provision with them. We all—whether married or single or widowed or divorced—need the revelation that our Maker is *our* Husband, too. He's not leaving any of us out; He has not forsaken us.

It's Easy to Forget

Even when we are resting in this hope through Yeshua, like the precious woman my pastor told me about, the enemy can steal away what we know. This happened to me after the death of my own mom. She suffered much in the last ten years of her life. She had conquered Hodgkin's disease but also suffered from several broken bones, heart ailments, high blood pressure, pre-diabetes—you name it, she just about had it. Yet she was there helping me to raise my children.

I literally was one of those in the "sandwich" generation. Since my parents didn't adopt me until their mid-40s, and I didn't have children until my late 20s and early 30s, I found myself with two small children on one end of the spectrum and my elderly mother in poor health on the other. Sometimes I didn't know if I was coming or going. Yet, she kept her mind and was able to help me with my little ones at the time, which was a blessing to me.

I remember the night when she went home to be with the Lord. As I found out from the hospital nurse that she was gone, I heard the familiar hymn ringing in my ears, saying:

Precious Lord, take my hand,

Lead me on, help me stand;

I am tired, I am weak, I am worn;

Thru the storm, thru the night,

Lead me on to the light;

Take my hand, precious Lord,

Lead me home.[3]

Yet despite all that I knew in Christ, about two weeks after her passing, I went into a deep depression. After all, I had just lost someone who had been with me 42 years of my life, who had helped me raise my children since my divorce, and who had been my friend and confidante. I was literally wallowing in all that was before me; I would now be raising two children alone.

After sinking in the muck and the mire for almost two weeks, I heard a knock on my door. A neighbor who loves the Lord stood there. He didn't even know that my mother had passed away, yet he told me, "The enemy is stealing everything away you know to be true." Wow! That hit me like a lightning bolt right between the eyes. He was absolutely right.

Later, I actually found a precedent for my seeming forgetfulness. At the start of the New Year, I began reading the Bible in a year using Young's Literal Translation. After Eve eats of the fruit, Jehovah God questions her about it and she says, *"The serpent hath caused me to forget..."* (Gen. 3:13 YLT). I had done the same thing! Of course, this verse is not a license to sin. Some may remember back in the '70s when Flip Wilson's popular television character used to quip, "The devil made me do it!" I'm not using this verse as an excuse, but noting that I am not alone in this experience of "forgetting" God's goodness.

During those two weeks, I was endlessly sliding down into the pit of depression and all the stuff that goes with that. I had been blinded to all the promises of Father God, but the precious Holy Spirit used my neighbor to open my eyes. My mother was saved; she had gone home to be with her Lord and Savior, and she was free from suffering. She is in her heavenly home rejoicing! I should have found comfort in that. Yet as my dad always said, "It's harder on the ones who are left behind." However, if we take our eyes off of ourselves and put them back on to Him, we will have that hope and peace that comes with the knowledge that one day we will not only be with our precious Savior, but we will also get to see our loved ones again. Thank You, Yeshua!

How many times have we seen it go the other way though? How many times have we seen a bitterness that develops over time in people who have no hope in Christ? Many of us have even seen and dealt with Christian brothers and sisters who chose not to let go of the hurt, anger, and resentment building up inside their lives. As the saying goes, *hurting people hurt people.* Some deal with it by building a wall around themselves, others by going after that next high or by jumping from relationship to relationship. It's almost like jumping into "default mode," stepping back into the familiar, the known, because the pain is too great.

Perhaps this has happened to you. Maybe you have developed a mean-spiritedness in your personality and have started treating others like you were treated in the past. You are hiding behind a defense mechanism. *Self* is now in control, not God. But this will lead you down a path of destruction. I have a friend who likes to say, "You'll be goin' around the same mountain again till Father corrects the situation." The precious Word says, *"For whom the Lord loves He corrects, just as a father the son in whom he delights"* (Prov. 3:12). Even though the correcting part is not fun, be thankful that He loves you enough to correct you! Know this, dear hearts: if you are struggling in deep sin right now, He doesn't love you any less!

THE RELATIONSHIP PROBLEM

Relationships are where most of us get out of balance, often getting into co-dependency. Too often we let our significant other take the place of our Abba Father. I have a good friend who said that a wise counselor once showed her how our relationships need to be like a triangle. Our Father

God is at the top, and the two people in relationship are at the two points on the bottom of the triangle. This applies to romantic relationships, as well as family relationships and friendships. As the two people grow closer to God (moving up the sides of the triangle) they also grow closer to each other. Isn't that a beautiful picture!

Father God doesn't want us out of balance. He knows it will affect our relationship with Him and with each other in an unhealthy way. Our God is a jealous God (see 2 Cor. 11:2)—jealous enough to want what is best for us. He wants to guard us and keep us in all our ways so we stay focused on Him and have that perfecting relationship in Him. From there, He will bring us into healthy relationships with each other. Sometimes this takes time, but I've seen it work. We may have the urge to run the other way, but we must not get distracted! The enemy would like nothing better than to pull you off of God's clear path.

Breaking Bitterness

I once ministered to an old soul who I have seen that hardness creep into. She had been widowed twice, and as I began to share the Lord Jesus with her, she turned me away, telling me she's "just a plain and simple gal." I did leave her a tract, a plan for the way of salvation, and then went on, continuing to pray for the Holy Spirit to come upon her life and for those bonds of bitterness and anger to be broken.

How about you? Do you need to break up your bitter heart, your hard ground? Hosea 10:12 advises, *"Break up your fallow ground, for it is time to seek the Lord, till He comes and rains righteousness on you."* You won't be able to step into the blessings of Christ unless you plow up those bitter areas of your heart and decide to walk in forgiveness. I don't know about you, but I want to reign in His righteousness. (We will delve further into His Word about *righteousness* in the last chapter.) I want to bask in His blessing. Ask our *Jehovah-Rapha* to plow up your desolate land, making it fertile once again (see Ezek. 36:34).

My name, *Mary,* in Hebrew means "bitter or a place in the desert—Marah" (Strong's #4785). It also means something more like "rebellion."[4] In the ancient days, the Hebrews gave their children names that meant something about their situation; it could mean something about their future or even their births. Their given name was an attachment to them—it followed them the rest of their lives. Neither meaning of my name adds a positive twist to my life. I wonder if Yeshua's precious mother Mary had to guard against a hardened and embittered heart once her Son, her first-born, was taken in the most brutal way.

I picked up an interesting little book several years ago called *The Prayer of Jabez.* It was a number-one New York Times bestseller written by Bruce Wilkinson. Jabez's name also has an interesting meaning—"pain" or "sorrow."[5] The famous prayer of Jabez is as follows:

> *Oh, that You would bless me indeed, and enlarge my territory, that Your hand would be with me, and that You would keep me from evil, that I may not cause pain* (1 Chronicles 4:10).

Just like Jabez, who wanted to rise above his name, I too have tried to guard my heart to keep it open to the risen Lord and to keep it open to others. I don't want to become bitter! I want to become better!

A New Name

After a particularly difficult situation, I was doing my best to not become hardened about it, and a very perceptive brother in the Lord came up to me and declared, "God has given you a new name."

I asked, "What is it?"

He answered with, "You will be able to tell me what it is in a few days... I asked Father God to reveal it to you."

Sure enough, within a few days, as I was pondering what it could be, I was reading about the different meaning of names and found that Mary means "Exalted of God."[6] At that point, I thought my name only meant "bitter."

I excitedly called up Brother David and said, "It's 'Exalted of God,' isn't it?"

He said, "Yep, that's it!"

Oh boy, did I *need* that! I wasn't feeling too exalted at the moment. To be honest, I was about to let the enemy drag me down into the pit (again). It's as if our Father, our heavenly precious Father, who wants to give us a hope and a future (see Jer. 29:11), whispered, "Hello, dear one. I want to give you a new name. It's still Mary, but it has a different meaning than the one you've been carrying around. It's not bitterness that you need to carry; your name means 'exalted of Me'!" Thank You, Father, for blessing us with new names.

Take the time to ask and find out your sweet and life-giving name that He has for you. Isaiah 62:2 says, *"You shall be called by a new name, which the mouth of the Lord will name."* He has a new name for you.

Remember the playground rhyme, "Sticks and stones may break my bones, but names will never hurt me"? Well, that's putting up a good front, and some of us may get hardened to those names, but the truth is that they do hurt. Some of those memories may stick with us for the rest of our lives. That's why parents should never call their children "stupid" or "idiot" and husbands and wives should not see who can out-do the other on the name-calling game. Since life and death are in the power of the tongue (see Prov. 18:21), we need to be careful what we call others, and we need to forgive those who have spoken wrongly to us. Speak life into your precious ones—not hurt, death, and destruction!

PRAYER NUGGET:

Precious Lord, thank You for Your Word today! We magnify You, El Shaddai, our All-Sufficient One! We thank You that You haven't given us a spirit of fear, but of power, love, and a sound mind. We thank You that You have given us the mind of Christ—Yeshua, who gives us strength. Thank You for freeing us from shame, loneliness, disgrace, and guilt.

Lord, we negate right now and take authority over the word curses that have been spoken against us, and forgive us, Father, where we have spoken wrong against others. Help us to be aware of our words and to speak life and not death.

*Thank You for Your love, Your perfect love that casts away our fears, our doubt. We love You, Father, and we thank You for sending Your perfect Son—for sending Your love to us. We thank You for giving us new names to walk in, Father! Thank You for giving us a hope and future. We thank You that Yeshua so loved us that He continued to walk toward that cross **for us!** Praise You, Father! We ask it all in Yeshua's mighty name and covered by His precious blood. Amen.*

ENDNOTES

1. Joyce Meyer, *Battlefield of the Mind* (Faith Words, 2002).

2. Rick Renner, *Sparkling Gems of the Greek* (Tulsa, OK: Teach All Nations, 2003), 73.

3. Thomas Dorsey, "Take My Hand, Precious Lord," quoted in Lynda L. Graybeal and Julie R. Roller, *Prayer and Worship: A Spiritual Formation Guide* (New York: HarperOne, 2007), 55.

4. *Christian Meaning of Names,* s.v. "Mary"; http://www.christian-meaningofnames.com/mary/; accessed August 4, 2011. Also, James Strong, *Strong's Exhaustive Concordance* (Peabody, MA: Henrickson Publishers), Greek #3137, Hebrew #4813.

5. *Strong's Exhaustive Concordance*, Hebrew #3258.

6. "Directory of Feminine Names," *Resources for Life,* s.v. "Mary"; http://www.resourcesforlife.com/library/names/feminine.htm#M; accessed August 4, 2011.

PERSONAL
Notes

_____

_____

_____

_____

_____

_____

_____

_____

_____

_____

_____

_____

_____

_____

_____

_____

_____

_____

_____

_____

_____

_____

_____

_____

_____

_____

_____

_____

Chapter Three

OUR LOVE—OUR HUSBAND

For your Maker is your husband, the Lord of hosts is His name;
and your Redeemer is the Holy One of Israel; He is called the
God of the whole earth (Isaiah 54:5).

Within the circle of mostly single friends I associate with, this is probably one of the Scriptures that we say and claim the most! *"Thy Maker is thine husband!"* (Isa. 54:5a KJV). Of course, we don't have to be single or even female to claim this one. The Holy Spirit does not distinguish us by our gender or marital status; we are all one in Christ Jesus (see Gal. 3:28). However, this verse does seem to ring out to the single person especially.

As Father God was speaking to the disobedient Israelites here, He was saying, "I am your Husband; I am your Redeemer." He was calling them back to Him. Individuals make up the people of Israel, and even if we are not Jewish, we have been grafted into God's family (see Rom. 11:16-24). Thus, we can see how He is wooing and calling every dear soul to Himself—the Holy One of Israel. Say to yourself, "He is *my* Husband!" Just as Jehovah God and the Jewish nation were Husband and Bride, so too are we, the Church today, betrothed to our Bridegroom—Yeshua. (See the parable of the 10 Virgins in Matthew 25:1-13.)

Some may wonder, *These words were written almost 3,000 years ago, so how does any of the Old Testament apply to me?* We find our answer in Hebrews 13:8, which says, *"Jesus Christ is the same yesterday, today and forever."* Yeshua, the Word who became flesh and dwelt among us (see John

1:14), doesn't change, dear hearts. His steadiness and His truth stand forever, and this gives us something to stand on.

HE *WANTS* TO BE *YOUR* HUSBAND

So what does all this mean to us personally? We all have different stories, yet this verse speaks to each of our circumstances.

Maybe you are married, but your spouse is not holding up his or her end of the bargain, and you are left in a loveless, contemptuous marriage. Some of the loneliest people in the world are those who are married but truly live alone. Maybe you've been newly divorced and you have children, yet your ex-husband is not paying child support regularly or even paying his half of their medical bills. Maybe you've been widowed, and you have little ones to raise by yourself.

Whatever the case may be, I beseech you to use this time to trust in your Maker, your Husband. Seek after Him in this trial, through this pain. He *wants* to be *your* Husband. Make sure you are looking to Him as your source and not to other people or other things. If you are using others as a crutch, you are becoming *a user*. You might end up catching yourself doing the same things others have done to you. Be careful if you find yourself falling into this pattern. I can guarantee you that Abba Father has something better in store for you if you will give your all to Him, if you give obedience to Him.

I speak from the perspective of one who was divorced at the age of 34 with two small children in tow. As I look back at what I've been through, I remember that when I sought after Him—my Maker, my Husband (not even knowing what Isaiah 54 said at the time, but just seeking Him)—and remained in obedience with right living, not seeking after other wrong relationships or worldly "stuff," I truly found that I was given so much more back.

I had a friend who always questioned why I didn't drink when we went out or why I didn't take men home. I tried to explain as best I could that I was living for the Lord. She just giggled and shook her head. Others will laugh; some will make fun, but I found that when I stayed the course with my Maker and Husband, when I stayed in His will, then I was given peace, joy, strength, and so much more. I think of the Scripture that says, *"Now to Him who is able to do exceedingly abundantly above all that we ask or think, according to the power that works in us"* (Eph. 3:20).

Take care of your precious Husband in your singleness. If you want to learn how to take care of an earthly husband (or wife), take care of your heavenly Husband first. I have found that when I minister to Him, all else is taken care of.

Will you get off track sometimes? Probably. Being single for most of your adult life will have you experiencing a lot of trials and temptations. When you are successful in those trials, it's like you are moving up a grade level. If you fail, you are held back, and it seems you'll have to experience that trial again until you do succeed. But if you can truly delight yourself in Him, then He will give you the desires of your heart (see Ps. 37:4). Our precious Maker/Husband always has so much more for us!

Hashem—"the Name"

As I was beginning to write this chapter, I opened my e-mail up to an article from the Elijah List, a daily prophetic publication.[1] The author cited Hosea 2:16 and discussed the Bride of Christ (that's us—*thy Maker is thine Husband*). I opened my Bible to those same pages in Hosea and was drawn to those sections that seemed to parallel what Isaiah 54 says. The prophet Hosea basically had the same motley crew of Israelites that Isaiah had to contend with, yet the Father continually loved them through their disobedience. (By the way, this has continually rung true since the time of Adam and Eve.)

I think the Stone Edition Tanach puts it best:

> *"And it shall be on that day"*—the word of Hashem ["the Name"]—*"that you will call Me Ishi* [my husband] *and you will no longer call Me Baali* [my master]*"* (Hosea 2:16).

Even in our sin, our very disobedience, Father God loves us so much that He whispers in our ears, "I am so much more than just your master. I am your Husband. I love you!" It is a continuous love story between our Husband/Maker and us, dear hearts!

Let's explore the name for God used in this passage—*Hashem*. Rabbi Laurie's wife, Dr. Martha, helped explain it to me this way. She said:

> *Hashem* translates as "the Name" because the name of God is never spoken except in prayer by the Jewish people. It is described as being "the sacred Four-letter name of God." In the Hebrew language God's name is written with the first four letters of a sentence, and the letters YHWH represent, "He was, He is, and He will be."

Even just saying this name makes me want to bow down in great reverence.

Stop and read the Book of Hosea, which shows the great love and mercy of our Lord. Just as Hosea brought back his wife, in spite of her adultery (representative of God's love for adulterous Israel), so did Father God forgive us and bring us back through the blood of His very own Son.

OVERCOMING ABUSE

I've heard that, for those who have been abused by their spouses, it's hard to relate to God as a husband because they were abused by the very ones who were supposed to love, honor, and cherish them the rest of their lives. I also know that those who experienced abuse by their earthly father or father-figure have a hard time relating to God as a loving Father. I can tell you one thing, dear ones. The wounding of our hearts by our own spouses, fathers, or other trusted people wasn't our Father's plan.

If we can keep it in perspective, we will realize that *hurting people hurt people.* Of course, the pain people have experienced is no excuse for them to hurt others. But as we start to see the hurt in their lives (looking at it from their eyes now), we can see how scared and hurt they must be to try and control others the way they do. Abusers tell themselves, "Hey, if I'm in control, then I'm not gettin' hurt."

Those who have been hurt by others—physical or sexual abuse, abandonment as a child, mental abuse by a spouse, even violence against them by a stranger (whatever the case may be)—are destined to repeat the abuse if they do not find healing. If they haven't forgiven those who abused them, then they will end up hurting their own mates, children, and even friends.

For this reason, you must be careful in your relationships, dear hearts. Watch out for people who have been abused but have not forgiven their abusers. *You* might end up paying the price for their hurts. If you are in that type of abusive relationship, try to get the person to go to a good, Christian-based counselor or pastor to get this worked through. You may even need some help at this point. Whatever the situation, you need to "walk through the fire" to get to the other side. If you just stand there and don't do anything, you are going to constantly get burnt!

Defining *Husband*

So what was Abba Father's original intent when He said the word *husband* in this passage? What comes to my mind, since I had a good role model in my own dad and I saw his day-to-day relationship with my mom and me, are words like *provider, decision-maker,* and even *fun-loving.* In my dad's case, he was a business manager, a risk-taker, a real ready-to-take-action-and-solve-problems type of guy. His example is what I think of when I think of the word *husband.*

I have the privilege of being able to attend a Shabbat (as in Sabbath-rest) service on Friday night less than an hour away from my home. This particular Messianic-Jewish congregation is called Adat Ariel—the Lion of God. They believe in Yeshua as the one true living God, as the Messiah who has come. All walks of life come to this congregation, from believer to nonbeliever, Jew to Christian, Baptist to Catholic to Pentecostal, and so forth. I've seen just about every religious group represented there. The leader of this congregation, Rabbi Moshe Laurie, received the Messiah in a dramatic "fulfillment of the Lord Jesus Christ" in 1982.

I asked my rabbi, "Just what is the definition of a husband in God's eyes?"

He answered, "You have Old Testament and New Testament, but it's the *full* testament in God's eyes. Ephesians 5 explains it very clearly, in that just like the Ten Commandments are actually eleven hundred if and thus's, the command of God is that, without reading the words directly, the man should treat the wife as Jesus treats the Church. The ultimate... the ultimate is that..."

He stopped to vividly point and added, "You see, you can't just answer what the husband needs to do without addressing the wife too. One is not conditional on the other, but they both need to be doing it or the marriage is not going to work."

He continued, "I'm sorry to say the wife usually winds up doing it more because men are notoriously..." and he stopped with a little smile, flipping his hand up in the air.

"Anyway," he continued, "basically how did Yeshua treat the Church? Well, the ultimate is He spread His arms and died, but more important, He gave His whole life from day one. He gave His whole life! I mean, God the Father knew that God the Son was going to have to go to earth and be miraculously born in the flesh, so the Lord knowing in the flesh He didn't have the power of God while on earth, dedicated Himself to the Father since childhood. He lived as a man, worked as a man, but the bottom line is, He dedicated His entire life."

Rabbi took a long breath and then said, "Now, when I counsel a couple, how do I tell this to a man who really doesn't want to hear it? Basically, what I say to them is: Look, she is right, even when she's wrong. The object is, the man must look upon himself as how the Messiah would treat the Church. Messiah treated the Church with compassion...and mercy...and kindness...even when they were wrong. Even when He—the Messiah—in the flesh, took the beatings, it's my understanding through Scripture that He never hit anybody. I mean, He could have...nothing could have prevented Him if He had really wanted to beat the snot out of anybody."

(By the way, don't you just love his candor!)

"The husband and wife are one, even though they live separately and not in each other's shadows. Spiritually they can't even fulfill the covenant of two or more. Scripture says, 'where two or more are gathered together'; they—the husband and wife—are only one spiritually. If a husband or wife needs prayer, it's good to pray for each other of course, but I suggest they get someone else to pray with them because they are not two. That's a very important teaching! The husband has to treat the wife as the Lord treated the Church. He treated the Church not just by spreading His arms and dying in the final moment, but he also dedicated His life, his physical life. The husband is the intercessor for his wife, the caretaker of his wife, the one who makes sure she lives and breathes and moves and that she's first whether he likes it or not."

Rabbi reflected a moment and continued, "Now it would be good if the wife would also obey the Scripture and understand it. As the Scripture says, the wife needs to treat her husband as the Church treats Jesus."

I interjected, "But the Church hasn't treated Him well!"

Rabbi nodded and lifted a finger, saying, "Most men will turn around and say, 'Well the Church submitted to the Messiah!'" Rabbi got animated here, "*No* they didn't! They [men] try to say '*you* [the wife] have to submit to me the way the Church submitted to the Messiah.' But as the Church had difficulty in serving, the intent of the Church's heart was to do so, and the intent of the wife's heart must be to be pleasing and obedient to the Word of God, through the Word of God to her husband."

Rabbi ended with, "The key—and this is where we tie it together—is let's say the husband is sitting here, trying to bring her to the understanding what is really right—not in his opinion, but what is based on the Word of God. He needs to try to be pleasing to her while bringing, as the head of the household, the Word of God as the primary obedience factor in their relationship. And the wife, in the understanding of the turbulence of the Church, attempts to the best of her ability, and the desire of her heart to be pleasing to her husband—in obedience to her husband, in just caring for him, as the Church in its way tried to care for the Messiah in obeying His Word, after He went back to sit at the right hand of God. Each one should both try to please God, and through pleasing God, are pleasing one another."

Rabbi looked up and said, "This would take volumes of books, by the way, to explain it all. But if each is trying to please God, based upon how they please each other—and there is not compromise—but giving and taking based upon the Word of God. Let me give you a for instance...The husband and wife are screaming at one another and then they both realize, 'Hey, this isn't pleasing to God.' It is not relevant who is right and who is wrong; what is relevant is, you need to ask, 'Is our conduct pleasing to God?' That's how I counsel couples, by the way, and the Word has every answer. In order to have a successful husband and wife relationship, both must be submitted to the Lord. What happens if one party is not submitted? Well, the other party has to keep praying and wait."[2]

That's the hard part, isn't it? To wait on that answer from the Lord as we have prayed and prayed and prayed our hearts out; then it's sit and wait time. I've heard it said, "Don't pray for patience! The Lord will have to test you then and make you wait to see if you have it!"

After our interview, I again got the chance to talk to Rabbi's lovely bride (as he calls her), Dr. Martha Laurie. I really wanted a chance to get in some girl-talk after some things that had happened in my life recently. I wanted her opinion on what so many singles seem to be chasing after—the "right one." She thought for a moment and then said, "You know, I don't believe there is such a thing. Back in the old days in the Hebrew tradition, and some even do it now, you had your marriages arranged for you. The families picked someone who thought they would be a good match. These marriages for the most part seem to work...as they learned to work together and love each other."[3]

"God always honors love," I said.

"Yes, He does," she agreed.

INFIDELITY

"For the Lord has called you like a woman forsaken and grieved in spirit, like a youthful wife when you were refused," says your God (Isaiah 54:6).

Looking at verse 6, I'm reminded of what infidelity does to a marriage. It hurts! The pain of being "forsaken" and "refused" leads to a deep grief of the spirit. This is exactly what Isaiah was describing.

I was actually one of the lucky ones (for lack of a better word). By the time I figured out what was going on, I was relieved. The marriage was so far gone at that point that I was like, *She can have him; I'm done.* We had even gone to a marriage counselor (a wonderful minister who was also licensed in counseling). He had us take the MMPI (Minnesota Multi-phaisic Personality Inventory) test. It was the "gold standard" of personality tests at the time, and the counselor wanted to see if there was any kind of disorder (bi-polar disease, schizophrenia, etc.) involved. Since there wasn't, the counselor's conclusion was that we were so far opposite each other that he didn't know if he was ever going to get us to meet in the middle. Even though there was too much "water under the bridge" at that point for us to get back together, it did motivate me to get out of an abusive marriage.

I feel somewhat blessed in that my experience was a gradual tearing apart. My heart goes out to the ones who get slammed by the sudden knowledge of an unfaithful spouse. My heart felt like it had a slow tear, but I know those who have had that initial shock, that sudden rip. My heart goes out to you if that has recently happened to you. Such wounds are hard to recover from, but I know many who have recovered. One friend told me, "If I hadn't had God to hang on to, I couldn't have made it." Father God became his spouse, his "Husband" (though it might be easier for the guys to think of God as their "wife" at this point).

Being refused, being forsaken, as this verse speaks of, creates a great hurt between a husband and a wife. To make matters worse, in my situation, I felt like my husband had not only cheated on me, but that he had cheated on my children too. I'm sure many can relate to this.

RELIVING THE PAIN

Sometimes writing or sharing about my experiences is like reliving all the terrible moments in my own marriage or life. It's like digging stuff up out of the grave again. I recently told someone, "If I never have to write or tell about that again, it will be fine with me." But then, over the weekend, Abba Father surprised me by showing how we can dig this stuff up to help others, and we don't have to go through a traumatic experience every time.

Some friends and I went to a church service to hear "Happy Jack" Burbridge speak. He was a former enforcer for organized crime back in the '60s. Listening to his story inspired me with the knowledge that Father can take those living in the lowest of gutters and turn their lives around. Burbridge was what most would call a "lost cause," yet God pulled him out of his life of crime and healed him so he could use his former area of brokenness to minister to others.

While there, I was given a copy of Happy Jack's book, *The Enforcer* (1980). In it, Burbridge speaks of having trouble with re-living "certain scenes from the past, and it was like digging up an old corpse." He spoke of coming out of one service "so overcome I had to walk around outside the church to get some fresh air." He went onto say "As I paced outside the church, the Lord spoke to me clearly, saying, 'Look, son, that man you talk about doesn't exist anymore. He died, and you are not that man." The Scripture he quoted often was, *"Therefore, if any man be in Christ, he is a new creature: old things are passed away; behold, all things are become new"* (2 Cor. 5:17 KJV). He said that "it breathed new life into him."[4]

That not only describes Jack's transformation but mine and yours as well. Have you noticed that Abba Father will meet you where you are? Whether you are a newborn Christian or a seasoned veteran, Father has the Word that you need at just the right time. Second Corinthians 5:17 was another *rhema* word for me. It spoke to my heart and started to heal this area that I was dealing with. Thank You, Yeshua!

Yes, this passage is the *logos,* which is Greek for the written Word of God. But sometimes the *logos* also becomes for us a *rhema*—it jumps out at us and speaks to our inner souls. This is what happened as I read Second Corinthians 5:17. I had read that verse before, but for some strange reason, I didn't think it applied to me. I figured that, because I have been a pretty good girl all my life and was raised in church, I really didn't need to become a "new creature." Oh boy, that was wrong! Romans 3 says, *"As it is written: there is none righteous, no, not one...for all have sinned and fall short of the glory of God"* (Rom. 3:10,23).

Second Corinthians 5:17 is such a powerful word. I am a *new creature* in Christ! *You* are a new creature in Christ! How did I read this and not understand it for so many years? I know many who have grabbed onto this Word from the very beginning of their walk with the Lord. Usually it's the ones who have dropped as far down in the pit as they can go who get a hold of this truth. Yet every Christian needs it! Let this word wash over you too so that old things may become new, so that *He* might sanctify and cleanse you by the washing of water by the Word (see Eph. 5:26). You are a new creature in Christ Jesus! Amen!

Prayer Nugget:

Precious Lord and Savior, thank You for the Word You have given me today. Thank You for being my Maker, my Husband, my Love. Thank You, Father, for desiring such intimacy with me that You tell me to no longer call You "Baali" (my master), but rather "Ishi" (my Husband). Abba Father, thank You for creating me to be a new creature through Yeshua! I breathe in that newness, so I can become one with You. Wash over me today with Your Word. Sanctify and cleanse me, most Holy One of Israel. Thank You for hope! Your love gives me strength and hope to carry on another day. I love You! In the precious name of Yeshua I pray, amen.

ENDNOTES

1. See www.elijahlist.com.

2. Rabbi Moshe Laurie, interview; http://www.shofarbetzion. com.

3. Dr. Martha Laurie, interview.

4. Jack Burbridge, *The Enforcer* (Dallas, TX: Acclaimed Books, 1980).

PERSONAL
Notes

Chapter Four

ONE WORD—MERCY

*For a mere moment I have forsaken you, but with great mercies I
will gather you* (Isaiah 54:7).

When I first read this verse, I thought, *What? Father, You said You
would never leave us or forsake us* (see Heb. 13:5). *What is going on here?
Why do You say that You have forsaken us?* This verse actually bothered me
so much I had to seek help from the Rabbi on it. It seemed like a contradiction to the rest of the passage, which tells me that our Husband is staying
the course.

That's just it. Just as a hurting husband would more than likely turn
away from his wife if she had been unfaithful (or vice versa), so too our
Redeemer, our Husband, had to turn from us—if just for a moment. It
hurts Him when we are unfaithful to Him. As Rabbi Moshe helped me
realize, "It's a parable!"[1]

LIVING *FORSAKEN*

Abba Father took me on an interesting journey as I wrote this book; it
seemed, at many points, like I was living it. Little did I know I'd be given a
trial on the way through it! I attended a Christian concert and ran across
someone I hadn't seen in a while. He asked, "So, how's your book coming
along?"

I just rolled my eyes and said, "Oh, I'm trudging through it."

He laughed and replied, "Aww—you're living your book then." Boy, am I ever!

As I'm in the "forsaken" part of this chapter, even living and breathing it, I asked, "Father, why can't I be living the good parts? The blessed and mighty and strong and favored parts?" Have you ever experienced this through a book or a song or even reading the Bible?

I have done different Bible studies over the years, and every time I did a particular study, it was like I was experiencing or living that part. When I studied the book *Experiencing God,* by Henry Blackaby and Claude King, that book lived up to its name! God's Word came to life when I read that one. I also read Beth Moore's book, *Get Out of That Pit,* a couple years ago. I was already in the pit, which is why I started reading it...to get out of that pit! I even had the privilege of teaching a book called *Woman, Thou Art Loosed,* by T. D. Jakes. I saw others experience parts of that book while we were studying it.

Over the course of the last two months, I've had people removed from my life—family members I thought I'd never be forsaken by. Looking at my cell phone, I realized that the number two, three, and four persons on my speed dial have been removed from me. The most important people in my life are gone; no wonder in this season I have felt a little depressed and overwhelmed.

"How did this come about?" I wonder. Some of it happened because of costly mistakes on my part, some because of other people's costly mistakes, and some as a mix in between. Of course, satan's job is to steal, kill, and destroy (see John 10:10), and he has played a part in this as well.

As I began to get hit with one thing after another, Father warned me of what was coming. It didn't make it any easier, but at least I had forewarning before the calamity hit. In the last chapter I wrote, "I feel somewhat blessed in that it was a gradual tearing apart [talking about the break-up of my marriage]. My heart felt like it had a slow tear, but I know those who have that initial shock, that sudden rip. Those are hard to recover from...."

It had been many years since I had a sudden heartbreak. Then, *WHAM!* My heart was shattered by someone who had told me, over the course of almost a year, that he loved me and could spend the rest of his life with me. Things had gotten a little tough, and we needed to let our heavenly Father make some corrections in the situation. It was nothing that time and Abba Father couldn't work out, and already He was faithful to begin doing it. Yet, instead of hanging in when the going got tough, I was told, "Oh, I've decided you're not the right one." That spirit of rejection—*ouch!*

To make matters worse, this is betrayal of the worst kind coming from those "in the church," people who I trusted. I experienced deep betrayal from ones I considered friends. We expect it in the secular world, but sometimes we unknowingly put our blinders on around "Church people." Then, by the time the blinders are off, it's too late. The cut goes even deeper because we trusted them even more, it seems. Most of us have experienced this, I'm sure.

CHASING OTHER LOVERS

When all this happened, I headed straight to the Word. If we can remember to do this in our times of pain, Father will answer us with that *rhema* Word that we need. I was asking, pleading, "Father, what do You have for me?" He sent me to Hosea 2, again. (I've been there before.) *Oh, this isn't good!* I thought. I knew what that chapter is about.

Hosea 2:6-7 says:

> *I will hedge up your way with thorns, and wall her in.... She will chase her lovers, but not overtake them.... Then she will say, "I will go and return to my first husband, for then it was better for me than now."*

What or who are your "lovers"? Have you started chasing after the bottom of the bottle again? Is it the love of money, the love of self? Are you still having trouble with lust issues, even pre-marital sex issues in your life? Maybe the lure of drugs is still urging you to "come back... come back." Praise God that He cares enough to "hedge up our ways with thorns"! Yes, we will be miserable when He starts to refine us in His refiner's fire. When I have sat in that fire, I have begged, pleading, "Lord, enough already!" He lovingly whispers, *"No, you're not ready to come out yet, My love. I'm watching over you...be still and know."* How about you? Have you chased after other "lovers" but forgotten the Lord?

One of my best friends (an awesome, praying warrior woman of the Lord) just recently experienced her son being arrested because he broke probation. He had gotten back into the drug scene. I remember praying with her that if it took jail or whatever to get him back in line, then so be it. It was just a matter of weeks until he stood before a judge who had mercy on him, and instead of giving him further jail time, he put him into a drug rehab center called Lifeline. This son told his mom recently, "Mom, this is the best thing that's ever happened to me." You see, our heavenly Father hedged his way in with thorns; He, Abba Father, threw him a lifeline.

THE REFINER'S FIRE

What does the phrase *refiner's fire* mean? Hundreds of books could easily be written on this subject. We get the phrase from Malachi 3:2-3:

> *He is like a refiner's fire and like launderers' soap. He will sit as a refiner and a purifier of silver; He will purify the sons of Levi, and purge them as gold and silver, that they may offer to the Lord an offering in righteousness.*

Isaiah 64:8 provides, *"You are our Father; we are the clay, and You our potter; and all we are the work of Your hand."* My wonderful editor and friend, Jennifer, added this insight:

> Pottery goes through a kiln, a fire that tests to see if the piece will break apart or stand. This fire also finishes the pottery by hardening it, something like making it more mature. In

this way, we are the pottery under the maturing fire of our Lord, the Consuming Fire.

We too must go through that fire to test us. Out of that fire will come our cleansing, our purification.

What does His fire need to burn off of us, dear ones? We must let that fire burn off our betrayal, our grief, our sorrow. The Word speaks of a godly sorrow that leads to repentance, which is the emotion we experience in the refiner's fire (see 2 Cor. 7:10). We must let Him burn off those wrong thoughts, those wrong issues in our hearts—the jealousy, the anger, the lust, the bitterness, the unforgiveness. Take it all, Lord Jesus!

As only He can and will, Father is turning our hearts toward that repentance we need, giving us that much-needed restoration, that much-needed hope. He wants us healed and whole. He wants us off of that "bottle," that "milk" we so desire. He is ready to give us "meat."

For everyone who partakes only of milk is unskilled in the word of righteousness, for he is a babe. But solid food belongs to those who are of full age, that is, those who by reason of use have their senses exercised to discern both good and evil (Hebrews 5:13-14).

THE VALLEY OF ACHOR

Returning to Hosea 2, we find this passage:

Therefore, behold, I will allure her, will bring her into the wilderness, and speak comfort to her. I will give her her vineyards from there, and the valley of Achor [which means "trouble"] as a door of hope; she shall sing there... (Hosea 2:14-15).

In these verses, God speaks of Israel and His relationship with the nation as a husband. (The "her" here is not gender-specific but is part of a marriage metaphor that applies to all of us who are in relationship with God.) It's also important to clarify we don't always have to be in disobedience to find ourselves in the wilderness. There are many (myself included) who have found themselves in a lonely place even when they were doing the right things. Regardless, this passage tells us that our place of trouble can be turned into a door of hope.

God says, in this trouble—our "valley of Achor"—in His hedging of our way, He is finally getting our attention. We have all been in that place where we have hit a wall (maybe several), and we can go no further in our own self, in our own futility (it seems the Israelites had this problem too). Abba Father is putting us in the wilderness for our own good, but *He* is going to comfort us there.

He is still showing us that He is our Husband, even if we have been disobedient. Yes, we must repent and turn if our sins have landed us in this place. If we do not, we will be unprepared for the enemy's attack. Our enemy likes to come when we are at our weakest, in the wilderness, just as he came to tempt Yeshua in His wilderness (see Matt. 4:1-11). Satan wants to steal our precious time with Father God and the healing that we will find there. Brave hearts, stand strong. If you can't stand, then sit, and if you can't do that, then lie down and throw a fit if you must! But don't be overthrown by temptations!

Look at what our Husband Redeemer says in Hosea 2:19-20:

> *I will betroth you to Me forever...In righteousness and justice, in lovingkindness and mercy; I will betroth you to Me in faithfulness, and you shall know the Lord.*

He says we *shall know Him*—speaking of an intimacy that only a husband and wife share. He's comparing the spiritual and emotional intimacy that we have with Him to the holy, naked intimacy of marriage. He is betrothing us to Him forever! And He's not finished with us yet! In the Valley of Achor, He will offer us the hope of truly *knowing* Him!

GREAT MERCY

Another aspect of the hope we find in our Husband is mercy. Verse 23 pops out at me: "*...I will have mercy on her who had not obtained mercy...*"

(Hos. 2:23). That's it! Some people are so wrapped up in themselves that we can't even obtain mercy from them, even when they are at fault too. Yet our heavenly Husband is not like that. This is a Word to hold on to, dear ones, a Word that will keep us clinging to Him. We can exalt in His mercy and faithfulness to us: *My Husband, My Righteousness, oh Lover of My soul! Praise to the King!*

Let's head back to Isaiah 54:7. It makes me cry as I read it: *"For a mere moment I have forsaken you, but with great mercies I will gather you."* As I read this, all I can think is, *What? Mercy—He's giving us mercy after we have been the ultimate unfaithful, disobedient backsliders to Him? Wow!* If only the human race could perform such a feat of mercy. *Webster's Dictionary* describes feat as a "deed of strength, skill, or courage."[2] I like that.

Rabbi Laurie has a copy of Noah Webster's First Edition Dictionary called *American Dictionary of the English Language,* which was originally written in 1828. It's definition of *mercy* is powerful. Oh my goodness! I'm quoting just a part of it here:

MER'CY, n. [Fr. Merci].

1. That benevolence, mildness or tenderness of heart which disposes a person to overlook injuries, or to treat an offender better than he deserves; the disposition that tempers justice, and induces an injured person to forgive trespasses and injuries, and to forbear punishment, or inflict less than law or justice will warrant. In this sense, there is perhaps no word in our language precisely synonymous with *mercy.* That which comes nearest to it is *grace.* It implies benevolence, tenderness, mildness, pity or compassion, and clemency, but exercised only towards offenders. *Mercy* is a distinguishing attribute of the Supreme Being.

The Lord is long-suffering and of great *mercy* forgiving iniquity and transgression, and by no means clearing the guilty. Num. xiv.

2. An act or exercise of mercy or favor. It is a *mercy* that they escaped.

   I am not worthy of the least of all thy *mercies*. Gen. xxxii.

3. Pity; compassion manifested towards a person in distress.

   And He said he showed *mercy* on him. Luke x.

4. Clemency and bounty. *Mercy* and truth preserve the king; and his throne is upheld by *mercy*. Prov. xxviii.

5. Charity, or the duties of charity and benevolence. I will have *mercy* and not sacrifice. Matt. ix.

6 Grace; favor. 1Cor. vii. Jude 2.

There are three more points after that, but I think we get the picture. My question is, are human beings even capable of this? When we couple mercy with that great word *love,* then yes, it is possible. God is love, that great, unending love who comes through even though a spouse has been unfaithful (enabling us to forgive) or a teenager tries and tests beyond our limits (enabling us to take the prodigal back). With God, it is possible.

In James 2:13 it says, *"For judgment is without mercy to the one who has shown no mercy. Mercy triumphs over judgment."* Thank You, Father! God has one word for us—*mercy*.

"With a little wrath I hid My face from you for a moment: but with everlasting kindness I will have mercy on you," says the Lord, your Redeemer (Isaiah 54:8).

This reminds me of marriage partners who are in a fight. After a fight, there has to be a cooling off period. *"With a little wrath I hid My face from you for a moment..."* It sounds like two lovers who are in a spat to me.

Soon after the experience of rejection that I mentioned earlier, my 21-year-old son—my firstborn—moved out of the house, and not on the best of terms, either. Suddenly I was dealing with rejection, the prodigal son, and the empty nest syndrome all at once. Then my beloved horse, one I had owned for over 15 years, died. As I meditated on Isaiah 54, I found myself thinking, *Father, You said "a little wrath." Do I have to get the whole enchilada here? If this is "a little wrath," I'd hate to see what a lot is!*

Yet this is our Lord speaking to us, our heavenly Father, our Husband. And after His "little wrath" comes His kindness, His forgiveness, and even that lovely word *mercy* again. *It's like a heavenly kiss!* He also identifies Himself as our Redeemer here. He has redeemed us, atoned for us, covered our sins for us, and bought us back from captivity with *His* own blood. It is time to open our eyes to see how passionately in love *He* is with *us*, dear ones!

LIKE A FLOOD

> *For this is like the waters of Noah to Me: for as I have sworn that the waters of Noah would no longer cover the earth, so have I sworn that I would not be angry with you, nor rebuke you* (Isaiah 54:9).

Verse 9 reminds me of Isaiah 59:19, *"When the enemy comes in like a flood, the Spirit of the Lord will lift up a standard against him."* Are you in a battle? Many of us may be in a battle, just coming out of one, or heading into the next.

I've heard it said that the comma in Isaiah 59:19 is in the wrong place—that it should be after the word *in*. That would make the Spirit of the Lord coming in like a flood, not the enemy. However, I'm not so sure about that; in the trials I've experienced, they always seem to come in like a flood.

The Hebrew language has no punctuation, which is why there is an argument on where the comma should be. As I mulled over this verse, a friend shared a dream she recently had. In the dream, she saw dark waters quickly cover over an area she was in. I too had felt like the enemy was coming in "like a flood," as the verse says. So I consulted Rabbi Laurie about it.

He asked, "What does it say in the Tanach?"

I told him, "It says, '...*for travail will come like a river, the spirit of Hashem will gnaw at them.*'"

He responded, "Listen, some like to call him a wimpy devil. The devil is not a wimp and does come in like a flood. Especially in this verse, the river *is* a flood because in that area there were no big rivers. However, the thing to remember is, greater is the spirit of the Lord which is in us." Amen!

Father promised Noah that there would never be another flood to cover the whole earth. So too He as our Husband has forgiven us. He is no longer angry with us. Even though we may be going through terrible trials right now, we can know that He will be faithful to His Word. The deep waters will not overtake us in our wilderness. I know that He *is* speaking comfort to me in my wilderness, especially *through* His Word.

THE RIGHTEOUS SURROUND ME

Another aspect of the Lord's comfort and provision for us in the wilderness is the friendships in the Body of Christ that He gives us. He has truly given me a circle of friends who I can call anytime. At times I have felt like I just about wore them out, yet, they continued encouraging, listening, and speaking with a kind word—more than that, the Word that I needed. Through these friends, God's word for that moment began to settle my mind, as well as the peace that comes from knowing, "OK, Father, You are in control of this even if I'm not."

I wrote in the dedication for this book, *"The righteous shall surround me, for You shall deal bountifully with me"* (Ps. 142:7). I like to say, "If you have a good friend to talk to, you don't need pills or a psychologist." Now, I'm not putting anyone down here, but I have found that by talking to good, solid friends and by pleading my case to the Lord, I'm able to regain my strength.

Make sure you are surrounding yourself with solid, nonjudgmental Christian friends (remember the importance of godly counsel). If they are judging you as you go through your trial—pass through your fire—then you don't need them in your life. It will be hard enough as it is, even without the naysayers! Think of Job, whose friends proved to be disloyal and unsupportive in the midst of his great suffering.

What does the Word say about how we are to serve each other? Look at Romans 12:3-8:

> *For I say, through the grace given to me, to everyone who is among you, not to think of himself more highly than he ought to think...For we have many members...but all do not have the same function... Having then gifts differing according to the grace that is given to us, let us use them: ...he who shows mercy, with cheerfulness.*

Good friends shouldn't judge—they shouldn't think more highly of themselves than they should or compare themselves to others. Rather, they should be understanding and merciful.

As I was living out those shattered hopes and dreams, often I would call someone to talk, but we would not get the needed breakthrough. It's not that that person was "off" in their ministering to me; I just didn't get the peace I needed (usually they are in their own trial at this point so we're praying for each other). Later I would call someone else, and Abba Father would use that friend at that moment to speak into my darkness—my wilderness. I would find my breakthrough! Perhaps it was timing. Or perhaps Father wanted to use a particular person (one who also needed encouragement) to minister to me so that I could tell him or her, "I'm better;

I'm finally getting peace now." Thus, that person would be blessed too, knowing God had used him or her. It's good for our souls to *know* we have helped another.

Many people have accountability partners. It seems to be popular among men's ministry groups in particular. As James 5:16 says, *"Confess your trespasses one to another, and pray for one another that you may be healed...."* Our *El Elyon*—our God Most High—knows that we not only need to confess our sins to Him, but we also need a confidant, a trusted friend who will not judge but who will listen and pray with us.

Also, as a certified facilitator through Turning Point Ministries, I know how important it is to talk with individuals who have been through the same things we are experiencing. We don't have to do this alone, dear hearts; others who have worn the same shoes can help us through. We've all heard it said, "Confession is good for the soul!" It is—as long as we're careful *who* we confess to!

Continuing on in Romans 12:9-15, we find God's definition of friendship:

Let love be without hypocrisy...Be kindly affectionate to one another...rejoice in hope...distributing to the needs of the saints. Rejoice with those who rejoice, weep with those who weep.

In the midst of my struggle, my precious friends were living out the Word, and their faithfulness to me made a magnificent difference. I suggest reading this whole chapter, which I call the brotherly love chapter, for yourself. It will show you how to properly treat others.

DEPARTING MOUNTAINS

For the mountains shall depart and the hills be removed, but My kindness shall not depart from you... (Isaiah 54:10).

So, dear hearts, have you had those mountains depart, those hills removed? Maybe your spouse took off for another lover. Perhaps you lost a job lately, and you have no prospects in sight. Maybe the life you envisioned with you and your children didn't turn out as you planned. Maybe the life of a loved one has been taken.

I'm sure you've heard it said, "Time heals all wounds." I think it's Yeshua who heals all wounds. Yes, time helps, but I know people who don't put their trust in the Lord, who don't seek Him in their pain, who don't have that hope. They don't seem to heal well (if at all), and they carry around that sorrow, bitterness, and disappointment all their lives. Go to Him, dear ones; press into Him, the only true Healer.

Through my recent time of trial, I heard of a place called The Prayer Center[3] only about an hour's drive away from my home. I went there just seeking Him. I encourage you to find a new place at times to seek the Lord. Sometimes it's a fresh word, an encouragement from people you don't know, or a fresh perspective that helps you break free. One day I grabbed the directions and just took off for my "adventure with the Lord," as a precious Christian brother would say.

A friend of mine encouraged me to go to The Prayer Center because she knew I needed peace and felt it would be a step in the right direction for me. When I got there, I discovered that I could relive Yeshua's journey to Golgotha at the Stations of the Cross. As I entered into the different-themed rooms, it seemed as if there is a different experience in each one. The Wailing Wall Room was a special place to pray and lay up my burdens. In the Open Heavens Room, I just felt led to lie down and soak in the awesome presence of Him. The Bethesda (which means "House of Mercy") Room had a soothing, beautiful water fountain as the focal point. I heard testimonies of people being healed there. One of the Scriptures painted on the wall really spoke to me: *"I have heard your prayer, I have seen your tears; surely I will heal you"* (2 Kings 20:5). Thanks and praise to our *Jehovah-Rapha,* our God who heals us.

The room that started to melt my ongoing unforgiveness, bitterness, and even wrath was the Ark of the Covenant Room. It happened to be the last room I entered, and I felt like I was prepared at that point. I didn't even know why. A Scripture painted on one of the walls was from Hebrews 4:16-17:

> *Let us therefore come boldly to the throne of grace, that we may obtain mercy and find grace to help in time of need.*

A CD has been playing in the Ark of the Covenant Room continuously for the last five years called, *I AM: 365 Names of God*. Some of the names of God are written in beautiful gold-colored scrolled writing on the wall. One was Jehovah-Shalom (God of our Peace). As I went over to light a candle under the name Jehovah-Shalom, the CD player happened to play at that exact moment, "Jehovah-Shalom, our Peace." Then I happened to look down at the shirt I had on and noticed that the word *peace* was written across it. Why I chose that shirt that morning, I don't know. But I was amazed by all the little nuances. Take notice of your little nuggets, your little nuances, too; that's God! I knew Jehovah-Shalom (my Peace-Maker) had met me there, and I started to have that peace wash over me, which was something I hadn't felt in a couple of months.

As I walked away from that room with God's peace, I wish I could say that it stayed with me through the rest of my trial. Not so, dear ones. After we encounter pieces of victory, satan gets even angrier at us and will throw something new at us. That's how we know we're reaching Heaven; it seems trouble (the Valley of Achor) is the norm now. We're making satan nervous as we stand on God's Word and start to get our breakthroughs. So he has to cause trouble; it's his job. *Remember, Father God will break through to us as long as we continue to break through to Him!*

THE NUMBER *SEVEN*

Have you ever come home to an e-mail, phone call, or message that turned your world upside down? I got one of those as soon as I came home from my journey to The Prayer Center. I knew it was time to write an email to address the recent situation. At that moment, a very prophetic friend of mine who I was sharing this with said, "Do not send it for seven days. Seven represents the number of completion." She's usually right about the timing of things, so I agreed. But with this e-mail came a new urgency, and I thought, *Send now!* Before I did, I happened to pull out some words and Scriptures that I had written down about this issue two months before. I had forgotten I had written most of them. The verse that absolutely jumped out at me was Psalm 119:164, *"Seven times a day I praise You..."* That number *seven* again. I knew I was to wait as instructed at that point (no matter how I felt—remember, obedience).

In our various trials and tribulations, we must remember to write down the *rhema* words we receive from God. In this instance, had I not done that, I would have missed Abba Father. That already-written Scripture made the correction for me. Habakkuk explains why:

> *I will stand my watch and set myself on the rampart, and watch to see what He will say to me, and what I will answer when corrected. Then the Lord answered me and said: "Write the vision and make it plain on tablets, that he may run who reads it"* (Habakkuk 2:1-2).

The very next day after I read the Scripture, *"Seven times a day I will praise You..."* I was in school teaching a class and began having disturbing images about this whole mess come into my mind, so much so, I literally felt my head and shoulders start to sink down. This continued about every half-hour, and I was sinking lower and lower. Finally, as I was being hit with another image, I heard the voice of the Holy Spirit whispering, "Why aren't you praising Me?" Then I knew—I was to praise Him seven times a day for seven days!

I happened to check my e-mail shortly after this realization, and the same friend who had told me to "wait seven days" had already sent me an e-mail talking about "Praising Him." I *knew* that it was confirmation. I texted my friends, asking if they would like to join in since I knew they were also in a trial. I explained that I felt led to praise Him seven times a day for seven days. I called it our "Praise Mandate." It sounds easy and even fun, right? I was thinking, *We get to praise our heavenly Father for seven days; we can do this.* I had no idea! Praise starts before a battle. It seemed like I had never seen the enemy throw more stuff my way than during that Praise Mandate. Satan doesn't want us to praise our heavenly Father—the Lover and Redeemer of our souls.

It was the most intense seven days I ever went through. I truly got to the point where I realized that I live and breathe and have my being in Him and Him alone. I felt He was literally giving me my breath as I was despairing in the loneliness, the pain, the hurt. About the third day, I had a moment in which I thought I had heard the Holy Spirit wrong. I was in such depression and despair that I thought, *This has to be the "sackcloth and ashes" stage. I need to be wallowing in my own self-pity here.* (Notice the word *self!*)

I got out my Bible, and Abba sent me another love letter. I opened right to where Jesus was feeding the 4,000 in Matthew 15:32-39. As I started reading, I was thinking, *What does this have to do with anything at the moment?* But then I read, *"And they said, 'Seven, and a few little fish'...And He took the seven loaves...they took up seven large baskets..."* (Matt. 15:34-37). There was that word *seven* again. To me, the number *seven* took on a great symbolism here; it is considered a number of *perfection* and *completion*. I knew at that moment that I was to rise up off the floor and praise Adonai! We must rise up out of those ashes, dear ones! Let Him perfect us; let Him complete us! Hallelujah!

This trial was one of great intensity. I knew in my heart that what people had shattered, only my Jehovah-Rapha could fix. There was such deep travail at one point (as, of course, it wasn't just one thing, but one thing on top of another) that I felt like, *This is it. I am going to have to finally go to the doctor and get some type of anti-depressant medication.* I'm not saying anything against this, but I have lived this out before (time and time again, actually), and I knew God could take care of all of my pain.

And once again, when I focused only on our Healer-Father, He gave me the strength to get through this fire.

I had also made the decision to *not* entertain any thoughts of suicide. I knew that once that evil spirit started to get a hold in my mind, I would not be able to make it. So I just fixed my mind on Him and kept quoting the mind Scriptures back at the devil (see Chapter 2). After the Praise Mandate was over, I knew victory was here. Thank You, Yeshua!

As I sat in a Sunday morning worship service just a few days after our Praise Mandate, the pastor said, "Turn to James 1:2." I almost jumped out of my seat as I knew this verse and had been considering where to put it in this chapter. The pastor started to read:

> *My brethren, count it all joy when you fall into various trials, knowing that the testing of your faith produces patience...let patience have its perfect work, that you may be perfect and complete* [the number seven!], *lacking nothing* (James 1:2-4).

Then the pastor added, "Don't give up, don't give up, don't give up!"

This verse is kind of an oxymoron, isn't it? Joy in our trials? I felt anything but. However, Abba Father is not too interested in our comfort. He is also not interested in the convenient. As a matter of fact, I have found that He likes to make it all the harder so that we learn to seek Him and then learn to let Him work it out. *He* is faithful to do it; He is faithful to complete us.

Are you one of those who has been despised, rejected, or unfairly judged—especially by those who have boards in their own eyes? (See Matthew 7:4.) If so, *"count it all joy,"* dear hearts, because Christ (even though He walked on this earth perfectly) was also despised, rejected, and beaten down just as you have been. *He* is just making you more like Him. To my brothers and sisters in the Lord who have prayed, fasted, praised, wept, and long-suffered—and still haven't seen what they thought would come out of that suffering, I say, "Hang on!"

THE WAY-MAKER

I was sitting on my bed one night asking Adonai, "Lord, can we do something here? I mean, I shouldn't have to keep going through this—this rejection, this hurt. I feel I'm ready to move on. What am I missing, Father?" As I pondered the few months prior, I turned on the radio and heard a woman speaking. It was as if she were me. I remember her talking about rejection after rejection, the heartache, and yes, the despair. It sounded as if she had asked Abba the same question I had just asked.

Then she said she had heard the Father say, "You know, if you'll just wait on Me to send you the one I have for you, you won't have to keep going through all this." She said she took those words to heart and did wait upon the Lord. I remember she said that after a couple of years she began to wonder if she had heard the Father right, as nothing seemed to be happening. Yet she kept waiting and did eventually meet her husband. Today they are very much in love and serving the Lord together. That encouraged me!

At that point, I asked the Lord through tears, "Wow, Lord, can You do that for me too?" It was only a night or two later when I started to get several words, actually little pieces of a puzzle that started to fit together. I know some people will think this is crazy, especially when we don't see the manifestation right away, but Abba showed me a revelation that just about threw me off my feet—something I wasn't expecting or could even imagine the remote possibility of. I had just come from a difficult situation, and now Father God was showing me an impossible one!

I began thinking, *Well, Father, did I hear You wrong in the last situation, as I felt You were working it all out at one point?* In that moment, the Holy Spirit gave me the realization that He *was* working it out, but that He also gives people free choice and free will. Once the other person changed his mind, Father put another plan in motion. This plan will be something bigger and better. My Husband had *"...by revelation... made known unto me the mystery...revealed by the Spirit..."* (Eph. 3:3-5). This plan will be something more than I could ever ask or imagine!

We must get to the point where we can trust Him for everything and anything! I had to get to the end of my rope to finally, *finally* ask Him, "OK, Father, what do You have?" Rejoice! Rejoice when we finally get to the end of ourselves—our selfish selves—and finally ask that question when all looks so bleak, as the darkness and brokenness surrounds us. In those revelations, our Plan-Maker, our Way-Maker says, *"For I know the plans I have for you, says the Lord. They are plans for good and not for evil, to give you a future and a hope"* (Jer. 29:11 TLB).

So, dear ones, if you have loved, if your heart was true, if you have done the right thing, if you stayed the course only to have your heart shattered, then *rejoice!* Lift up your heads, brave hearts, for we know the one, and only one, who lifts up our heads (see Ps. 3:3).

COVENANT OF PEACE

The second half of Isaiah 54:10 says:

Nor shall My covenant of peace be removed," says the Lord, who has mercy on you.

"My covenant of peace..." Let that soak in for a second. While writing, I kept hearing the word *covenant* over and over. *Webster's* defines *covenant* as "agreement; writing containing the agreement; contract, bargain."[4] Adonai was covenanting to the Israelites in this passage not only as their marriage partner—*"Thy Maker is Thine Husband"*—but also as their *Peace Maker.*

Months after the trials I described earlier, my *Husband* was truly showing up as my *Peace Maker.* When we can step back from our situations (usually months or even years later), we are finally able to realize our own part and responsibility in our situations—whether good or bad. The Bible says our righteousness is as filthy as rags (see Isa. 64:6). Yes, we are washed clean by the blood, but even blood-bought Christians need an attitude adjustment once in a while.

I realized that over the course of that year I definitely had not been at my best for the Kingdom. I had let the pressures of a daughter who never returned home (yet!) get to me. I had let financial and life pressure wear me down. I had been overwhelmed by circumstances. I am still believing, but I'm also in the "waiting on the promises" part. Proverbs 13:12 has some wise words on this—*"Hope deferred makes the heart sick...."* I know this to be true. But there is still hope. Look at how the verse finishes:*"But when the desire comes, it is a tree of life."* Adonai knows that our hearts grow weary in the waiting, and He Himself encourages us that when our desire comes, we will spring up again.

Look at Abraham. He believed that Eliezer of Damascus would be his heir rather than one of his own offspring. Father God had a different idea and said, *"This one shall not be your heir, but one who will come from your own body..."* The Bible records, *"And he* [Abram] *believed... and He accounted it to him for righteousness"* (Gen. 15:4-6).

Abram believed, yet what happened? After many years of waiting, he and Sarai decided to take matters into their own hands, and Ishmael was born through the Egyptian handmaiden, Hagar. Ishmael was blessed, as the Word says, but he was not the promised heir. After all that, *El Roi,* the God Who Sees, sent the promise—Isaac—14 years later!

Most of us do just what Abraham did. We get tired of the wait and end up taking matters into our hands. Most times, we end up with something we never should have had in the first place. Look at Moses. Even he got tired due to Israel's disobedience, and in his frustration, he ended up striking the rock twice, which was against God's command (see Num. 20:11). This understandable act left him unable to enter into the Promised Land.

Thankfully, Father God had compassion on us enough to send His very own Son, Yeshua, who now sits at His right hand praying and interceding for us when we have fallen down, even if it happens again and again! Through Him and Him alone, mercy and peace are coming for the ones who have not obtained mercy. He is the lifter of our heads!

PRAYER NUGGET:

Adonai, I praise You. I praise You in the midnight hour. I praise You when all hope is gone. I praise You when I rise and when I fall. I praise You in the morning. I praise You in the evening. I praise You and You alone, Father.

Help us to remember during those long, dark nights of our souls that You are here. You haven't left us or forsaken us. Hedge our way up for our own protection, Abba, and talk to us softly, sweetly in our wilderness. We want Your love letters to us, Yours and Yours alone. Help us to not seek the wrong things through these trials, but to seek only Your face—our Love, our Husband. Thank You for bringing us through to hope, restoration, and healing.

Thank You, Abba Father, for Your great and unending mercy toward us. Help us to receive Your mercy toward us, and to be able to extend that same mercy toward others. Thank You for making our shattered hearts whole once again so that we are free to move ahead for all that You have for us. Adonai, we thank You for giving us a hope and a future. Thank You for being our marriage partner and for granting us peace. Thank You, Abba, that where we once walked in shame, You have lifted our heads. In Yeshua's precious and mighty name we pray, amen!

ENDNOTES

1. Rabbi Moshe Laurie, interview; http://www.shofarbetzion.com.

2. E. T. Roe, *Laird & Lee's Webster's New Standard Dictionary of the English Language.* (Chicago: LL. B. Laird & Lee, Inc. Publishers), 192.

3. The Prayer Center's website is http://www.theprayercenter.us.

4. E. T. Roe, *Laird & Lee's Webster's New Standard Dictionary of the English Language.*

PERSONAL
Notes

Chapter Five

THE GRACE CHAPTER

O you afflicted one, tossed with tempest, and not comforted... (Isaiah 54:11).

For by **grace** *are ye saved through faith; and that not of yourselves: it is the gift of God: not of works lest any man should boast* (Ephesians 2:8-9 KJV).

I quote Ephesians 2 here because this is Chapter 5, and the number *five* has the meaning of "grace." My theme in this chapter is my healing testimony ("O you afflicted one"), and as I started writing, I heard the phrase, "you have been saved by grace through faith." My healing definitely did not come from anything I did; it was all Him.

Not by works of righteousness which we have done, but according to His mercy He saved us, through the washing of regeneration and renewing of the Holy Spirit, whom He poured out on us abundantly through Jesus Christ our Savior, that having been justified by His grace we should become heirs... (Titus 3:5-7).

Thank You, Yeshua!

I am definitely a grace girl. How about you? Are you a person of grace, or do you constantly beat yourself up under law? I identify with people who have been beaten, downtrodden, lied to, used, and broken. I can relate to those who have made some mistakes—lots of them. We are people of grace whom Father God can so use some day, maybe even today! I talked with a friend recently about grace. She said, "Boy, I have seen that in a cousin of mine. When he first came to the Lord, he was on fire and just loved the Lord and loved people. Then he became indoctrinated with church law, and instead of loving people, he became more involved with quoting law, and it's like the love and the fire left him."

Such people self-righteously say, "Well, I don't do that," and "I don't do this," yet in their own pride they point the finger and judge others. These people get all angry and indignant as they try to point out other people's faults. This falls into the "religious spirit" category.

That is not how we are to be. Rather, we are to gently help others and then let it go and let God. Galatians 6:1-4 backs this up, saying,

> *Brethren, if a man is overtaken in any trespass, you who are spiritual restore such a one in a spirit of gentleness, considering yourself lest you also be tempted. Bear one another's burdens, and so fulfill the law of Christ. For if anyone thinks himself to be something, when he is nothing, he deceives himself. But let each one examine his own work...*

Instead of the hissing sound of condemnation, I hear the apostle Paul speaking nothing but soothing, gently spoken words. We must restore one another with gentleness, lest we fall and need to be lifted up ourselves. Correction *must* be tempered with love, dear hearts—His love working through us to help others.

When we ask for and allow our Maker to restore us, He will do His perfecting work in our lives. *El Shaddai*—Who is Enough—tells us to:

> *Work out your own salvation with fear and trembling; for it is God who works in you both to will and to do for His good pleasure* (Philippians 2:12-13).

Grace is not an excuse to sin. Instead, grace should be empowering us to overcome it! Paul takes care of this issue in Romans 6:1-2—*"What shall we say then? Shall we continue in sin that grace may abound? Certainly not!...*" Look over Romans 6-8. Read and meditate on these truths about grace (there may be a test afterward—literally).

I looked up *grace* in Webster's 1828 dictionary, *American Dictionary of the English Language,* as well. Compared to *mercy's* nine definitions, *grace* has 20! Here are some highlights:

GRACE, n. [Fr. Grace...The primary sense of *gratus,* is free, ready, quick, willing, prompt, from advancing.]

1. Favor; good-will; kindness; disposition to oblige another; as a grant made as an act of *grace.*

2. Appropriately, the free unmerited love and favor of God, the spring and source of all the benefits men receive from him.

   And if by *grace,* then it is no more of works. Rom. xi.

3. Favorable influence of God; divine influence or the influence of the spirit, in renewing the heart and restraining from sin.

   My *grace* is sufficient for thee. 2 Cor. xii.

4. The application of Christ's righteousness to the sinner.

   Where sin abounded, *grace* did much more abound. Rom. v.

5. A state of reconciliation to God. Rom. v. 2.

6. Virtuous or religious affection or disposition, as a liberal disposition, faith, meekness, humility, patience, proceeding from divine influence.

7. Spiritual instruction, improvement and edification. Eph. iv. 29.

8. Apostleship, or the qualifications of an apostle. Eph. iii.8.

9. Eternal life; final salvation. 1 Pet. i. 13.

10. Favor; mercy; pardon.

There are still ten more to go! (By the way, I smiled when it listed *grace* as prayers before a meal.) I'm sure we are getting the picture that our Jehovah God has covered it all for us. It is so much more than we ever deserve. I can't even wrap my brain around it! I always say that there are not enough words in the English language for us to be able to express our gratitude toward Him.

O AFFLICTED ONE

"O you afflicted one, tossed with tempest, and not comforted..." (Isa. 54:11).

As we turn our attention back to this line in Isaiah, Father God is trying to comfort the nation of Israel. This verse actually comes as close as possible to describing my life about six years ago. I was getting so sick at that point that I called in the executor of my estate to get my affairs in order. To fully understand the scope of this, I have decided to back up all the way to my early teen years. This is to give someone hope when he or she feels there is none.

For some reason, I have been struck with nearly every major female issue one could have. From the start of my period in my early teens, it seemed I "had it all." Over the course of time, endometriosis, cystic ovaries, and fibrocystic breast disease encompassed my life. I have also had an issue with an "uncooperating" back. The doctors call it scoliosis, but I don't claim that!

"Death and life are in the power of the tongue, and those who love it will eat its fruit" (Prov. 18:21). We must be careful how we word things. I learned this great lesson from Pastor Darlene Bishop after attending a Judy Jacobs seminar in Nashville a few years back. Pastor Bishop has some great healing testimonies that she shares. And I know that if Father God

is willing and can do it for her and her family, then He can and is willing to do it for us too. As Pastor Darlene would say, "Just *BELIEVE!*" She has an acronym the Holy Spirit gave her for BELIEVE—Because Emmanuel Lives I Expect Victory Everytime![1] Amen!

THE NATURAL ROUTE

When I was in my late 20s, due to a series of horse riding accidents, several other injuries, and a stressful marriage, my back really decided to flare up. Medical doctors at the Mayo Clinic were telling me that I had a "smidgen of multiple sclerosis," while the chiropractors were saying, "You don't have MS. Your spine is leaning over to the right, pushing on your muscles and nerves and causing your leg tingling and double vision." I even had to wear an eye patch at one point.

One doctor at the Mayo Clinic said, "You know, you will be in a wheelchair by the time you are 35; when you get really bad, come in and I'll give you some drugs."

I am kind of a natural health nut, so I sat up (more worried at the drug statement at this point, than the other) and said, "Drugs? What kind of drugs?"

He replied, "Oh you know, some cortisone, steroids."

Not only do I prefer the natural route, but I can also be somewhat stubborn (I prefer to think of it as having personal resolve); I knew right then and there that I was going to follow a different path.

At that time, I was a born-again Christian and had been for at least 10 years, but I didn't know much about claiming healing by Yeshua's stripes. However, Father had given me insight on learning how to take care of my body better because *"Your body is the temple of the Holy Spirit who is in you..."* (1 Cor. 6:19). So I started on a healthy regime of eating organic when I could, incorporating massage with spinal adjustments, and getting on an exercise program to make my back stronger.

Let's just say all of it is still a work in progress. I am now two decades past the doctor's timeline for being in a wheelchair. I am blessed to have my own cleaning business, and I still ride horses, bike, walk, jog, and so forth. I am also still praying for a total healing—to be made whole! Oh, yes, I *BELIEVE* it! Thank You, Jesus!

HITTING 40

Things seemed to settle down in all my health issues till I reached the age of 39. Then, all the female issues began to worsen, and a couple months after my 40th birthday, I was diagnosed by a naturopath as having a Candida yeast condition. This is a chronic type of infection that runs throughout the whole body. It seemed to age me overnight. I began seeing a chiropractor and acupuncturist who also worked with herbal medications, and he did some amazing work. We eventually got rid of that awful infection, but it seemed that as soon as we had healing in one area, another problem would pop up. It was becoming a vicious cycle.

Fast forward a few years to 1993. By that time I was going to two natural medicine doctors. One was a Chinese-trained medical doctor, and she was able to get specific Chinese herbal medicines that I needed. The other was the chiropractor I mentioned earlier.

Genesis 3:18 says, *"And you shall eat the herb of the field."* I'm not saying that taking pharmaceutical drugs is wrong (though looking up *pharmakeia* in Strong's concordance is rather eye-opening). However, I had come to realize that my sensitive system could not handle traditional medicine. When I explored that route years before, traditional medical doctors wanted to put me on hormone pills. Yet I've had a sister die of breast cancer and a grandmother die of ovarian cancer. Taking hormones just is not an option for me. I realize that not everyone agrees with my perspective, and my desire here is not to argue about it but simply to share my experience.

Initially the herbals were all helping, but after a year or so, it seemed nothing was helping and my condition was worsening. I finally broke down and went to a medical doctor. As this doctor started some exams and testing, she said that due to the symptoms I was having, I would probably need surgery—a total hysterectomy. Then she said, "Don't be surprised if a round or two of chemo follows after that."

At that point, my natural medicine instincts kicked back in and I realized that I needed a different course of action. I was not going to do surgery. I kind of like the body parts the good Lord gave me, no matter how stubborn they were being. So I went to the local health food store and researched some different herbals and then went back to my chiropractor. I only needed a couple of different herbs added to my regime.

PREPARED TO DIE

However, the fact was, I was ill—so ill that I called in the executor of my estate. I realized that if things didn't improve, I was going to need help in getting my affairs in order. I was not feeling well enough to do it myself. When my executor/friend Toni walked in my house, she said, "I can tell you've been sick. I've never seen your house in such a mess!" She got busy lining up the house and my paperwork and even making sure I was taking my herbals.

Within three days of getting on the new natural meds, I was feeling remarkably better. Plus, it was the first time in well over 20 years that someone was taking care of me. I actually relaxed and felt good about it.

After about a month or so, my health seemed to be improving. But then I was involved in a terrible accident that totaled my two-year-old truck! I was t-boned by a guy talking on his cell phone and driving 65 mph. (I was barely going over two miles an hour.) I was following a friend to his house to help him with moving. Next thing I knew, I was being pushed down the highway sideways and ended up in a ditch. All my doors were jammed, so I climbed out the driver's side window.

The police were trying to get me to go to the hospital, but I knew I was going to be OK. One made the comment, "Ma'am, we have never seen an accident this bad where the passengers didn't go to the hospital." I explained that my friend would take me home and watch me and that I would make an appointment that day to see the chiropractor. Somehow, I walked away with only a mild to moderate side whip-lash. The other driver was unhurt. We both had a lot to be thankful for. I like to say our guardian angels worked overtime that day.

About a year later, in the spring, I began to notice that I was starting to feel worse again. This time, I went downhill fast. If the good Lord didn't intervene, I felt I would be gone in about three weeks. I was only able to muster up the strength to work one half-day per week at a local school as a teacher's aide. I started to think, *Father, You are either going to heal me or take me home.* At this point, I felt my life duties were over. I had recently lost my mother, my two children had moved to their dad's, and a man whom I thought I was going to marry had left.

Some may be wondering, *Why didn't you just go to the doctor?* Beside the reasons I mentioned earlier, I knew that surgery would be their course of action, and I really had no one to take care of me after surgery. I also was just about financially wiped out and without good insurance. I did not want to leave my children without anything at all.

In many ways, I felt my role as a mother had been completed. I had seen both my children accept the Lord Jesus Christ as their Savior, which was my biggest desire for them. My son had gone forward at church a few years before to accept Yeshua, and my daughter had gone forward at a Billy Graham Crusade about a year after that. I had also spent the last 10 years taking care of my ailing mother. Now that she was gone and my kids had moved away, I truly felt my work here on earth was done.

THREE-PART PRESCRIPTION

One night, I went to bed feeling awful, thinking, *If this is how life is going to be, I'm done. I want to go home.* However, that very night I woke up feeling so sick at 2:00 A.M. and started to plead my case to the Lord. I remember saying something like, "Father, You can have me if You want me, but You know, this is not what Your Word says! Your Word says that by Your stripes, Jesus, I am healed." Then I got in the Word, and I begged, pleaded, declared, and wrestled all night. It reminds me a bit of Genesis 32, where Jacob wrestles with God. I knew the struggle was on.

At 7:00 A.M., I got up to get ready for work, and all I could say was, "Help me, Jesus! Help me, Jesus!" Since I lived close to the school where I worked, I walked there that morning, saying with every step, "Help me, Jesus! Help me, Jesus!" In between classes, I wrote the words, "Help me, Jesus! Help me, Jesus!" on the blackboard. Then I would erase it, rewrite it, and erase it again until the kids came back to class.

I went home at noon to warm up some soup and go to bed. However, I got a call from someone at my church (we didn't know each other very well then). She asked if I would meet her for lunch. I could be on my death bed, but I still wouldn't miss a social call. So I turned off the stove and headed to Logan's Steakhouse. I sat down with my new friend, Sonja, and her daughter, Jessica, and proceeded to tell them all that was going on.

Jessica is a precious child with Down's syndrome, and she is very patient. I was telling Sonja that I hadn't gotten much sleep the night before and that, as I woke up, I realized that I was not going to live much longer. Sonja asked me what time I woke up, and I said, "Exactly two o'clock." Sonja about jumped out of her seat and excitedly exclaimed, "That's exactly the time the Lord woke me up!" She then gave me two pages of healing Scriptures and told me the Lord had showed her three things I was sup- posed to do. First I was to read those Scriptures three times a day, starting with this verse:

> *As for me, I will call upon God, and the Lord will save me. Eve-*
> *ning, morning and at noon will I utter my complaint and moan*
> *and sigh, and **He will hear my voice**. He has redeemed my life*
> *in peace from the battle that was against me [so that none came*
> *near me], for they were many who strove with me* (Psalm 55:16-
> 18 AMP).

I will include the rest of the healing Scriptures at the end of this chapter.

Second, she felt I was supposed to go see the new Mel Gibson movie, *The Passion of the Christ*. It hadn't been out long, and I hadn't seen it yet (though she didn't know that). In about a week, I went to see the movie. It was extremely hard to watch at times—to think He took those beatings, those stripes for us! He willingly did it; even while we were yet sinners, He died for us (see Rom. 5:8). I don't think we'll ever really know the cost of that.

Third, I was supposed to take daily communion. I decided to take it with actual red wine and unleavened bread. I wanted to do it as Yeshua would have done it over 2,000 years ago. As I was instructed to take it daily, I decided to take the communion by myself in the evening. I followed the Scriptures in Matthew 26 about the Lord's Supper.

I thought I would have a nice, peaceful, and quiet time following the instructions and waiting on the Lord. Not so! Just as in the Praise Mandate (which I discussed in Chapter 4), the fight had begun. We see this time and time again in the Bible. Look at Genesis 12. Abraham was told to get up and "pitch his tent" in another land. Reading further, we see that there was a *famine* in that land. I'm sure Abraham is thinking, *Lord, have I heard You right?* How about David? He was told by Jehovah that he would be king; then David found himself running for his life (see 1 Sam. 19). Or look at Yeshua. After He was baptized by John the Baptist, the Spirit of God rested on Him in the form of a dove, and He heard a voice from Heaven say, *"This is my beloved Son in whom I am well pleased"* (Matt. 3:17). Next thing we know, Yeshua is in the desert getting tempted and tested by the devil.

LYING VOICES

We have all heard (usually) well-meaning people say to someone who is sick, "It's because of sin you are sick!" This just makes my blood boil! Well, what the heck happened to Job then? The Word says that he *"was blameless and upright, and one who feared God, and shunned evil"* (Job 1:1), yet he was afflicted. When we get to feeling sorry for ourselves because of all that's happened in our lives, there's nothing like reading the Book of Job to give us some perspective. It works for me! I get to feeling better really fast.

Unfortunately, we are all going to get sick at one time or another. Yes, sin did enter the world because of Adam and Eve. But that doesn't mean that every sickness is a result of sin. People who say such things should be careful with the way they speak. Next time it might be them getting sick. Listen, dear ones, sickness might be a test from God (as in Job's case), or it might be caused by our own sin. If that's so, we must seek Jehovah's guidance and He will show us what we need to repent of (it might be something from many years past).

Too often we have focused on sin as the cause for sickness, while forgetting the time when Jesus saw a blind man from birth. His disciples asked,

"Master, who did sin, this man or his parents, that he was born blind?"

Jesus answered, "Neither hath this man sinned or his parents: but that the works of God should be made manifest in him" (John 9:2-3 KJV).

Then *Jehovah-Rapha* used it for His glory as He healed him!

TURBULENCE

I called Sonja after a few days of following her plan and complaining, "It's getting worse. I'm feeling worse. I can't do this!" I was even starting to have symptoms again of things that I had been healed from by the chiropractor/acupuncturist years earlier! Later I realized that I needed to go through this because *"If the Son therefore shall make you free, ye shall be free indeed"* (John 8:36 KJV). I wanted and needed to be free! Hallelujah!

In my complaining (sorry, Father!), Miss Warrior Sonja would spring up and say, "Oh goodie! You're touching Heaven, and you're making the devil mad; that's why it's getting worse. Hang in there; don't stop.

Whatever you do, don't stop now." I didn't have the strength to argue, so I just kept at it.

Then the real battle began. After about a week, satan started going after my mind. Remember what I wrote about the mind in Chapter 2. Now my mind was being attacked. It got so bad that I ran to the medical doctor for some type of anxiety pill. I had to pay for everything out of pocket, though, so when the pharmacist said, "That will be $200" (it was some exorbitant amount like that), I just turned around and walked out. I was thinking, *Just what I need to do. I have no money coming in, and now I'll have more anxiety trying to find the money to get the pills.* I scrapped that plan.

After three weeks, I started getting words like "the snare of the fowler has been broken," or a letter from some ministry would come in the mail with big bold letters saying, "You're healed!" on the front cover. Yet, I didn't feel healed; I didn't really feel well at all.

I headed to church that Sunday morning and walked by a man I didn't know. He had only been going there about two weeks. As I walked by him, he pointed his finger in my face, and as I looked up he said, "You've been healed; you just don't know it yet." I was thinking, *Well, if I've been healed, I don't feel like it. I feel awful. If this is what "healed" feels like, I would hate to see it when I'm sick.* It was as if he read my mind. He said, "No, really! You have touched Heaven. God has heard your prayers."

Second Kings 20:5 says, *"I have heard your prayer, I have seen your tears; surely I will heal you...."* Wow! *He* did hear my prayer, and *He* did see my tears, and *He* did surely heal me! Thank You, *Jehovah-Rapha*.

As I sat in service that Sunday morning, I thought about what my brother in the Lord had just said. I can't say I had some great faith. I always thought healings were for "someone else," but I didn't think Yeshua would possibly want to heal me. The "I'm not good enough" syndrome would always start in. To be honest, we are all "not good enough." He heals us because of His grace.

All I knew was that I had walked out what I had been told to do. It wasn't something stupid or anything. I mean, I wasn't told to jump off a bridge or go hurt or maim someone (and if you are then you are following the wrong god!). I knew it was from God, and I obeyed. There were times when people were healed instantly throughout the Old and New Testament. The Israelites were instantly healed of snakebites when they looked upon the brass serpent (see Num. 21:8-9). The brass serpent was a representation of Jesus being lifted upon the cross (see John 3).

However, my experience was more like that of the blind man I spoke about earlier who was healed in John 9.

> [Yeshua] *spat on the ground and made clay with the saliva; and He anointed the eyes of the blind man...and He said, "Go, wash in the pool of Siloam...." So, he went and washed, and came back seeing* (John 9:6-7).

I had to walk out my faith, walk out what He had shown me. It may be that way for you too.

Another one of my favorite Scripture passages about this is in Second Kings 5. Naaman, the commander of the Syrian army, had leprosy and went to the prophet Elisha to get healed. Elisha sent a messenger to tell Naaman to *"Go and wash in the Jordan seven times..."* (2 Kings 5:10). This made the commander furious because he wanted to wash in his own country's rivers. However, after his servants spoke to him, he went and dipped in the Jordan as first instructed. He came away cleansed and restored! Amen! I can relate to that.

As the words *you've been healed* started to sink in, I thought, *Well, if I've been healed, I better get to my chiropractor then.* I was on all these different herbal medications, and I realized that I better be getting off of them. About three days later, I went in to see the chiropractor and didn't tell him much of anything except that I felt there had been a change. As he started his exam, he kept saying, "Well, you don't need that herbal anymore." It ended up that he took me off every herbal medication I was on and proclaimed, "You are the healthiest person who has ever walked through that door!" Then he thought for a moment and said, "Well, no, I take that back; there's a preacher woman who comes in here, and she's pretty healthy." I just looked at him and humbly said, "Well, Jesus did it." And he had—over 2,000 years ago. Thank You, Yeshua!

GOOD THINGS COMING

Behold, I will lay your stones with colorful gems, and lay your foundations with sapphires. I will make your pinnacles of rubies, your gates of crystal, and all your walls of precious stones (Isaiah 54:11-12).

We have been afflicted, have been in the tempest and tossed all about, yet suddenly our Husband Redeemer says, "Wait! I have good things coming for you!"

Gems and precious stones have symbolic meaning within the Bible. In other translations, a different stone or two is listed; apparently there has been some confusion translating from the Hebrew into English. For the sake of simplicity, I am going to stick with the New King James Version.

Sapphires

First, Isaiah lists sapphires, *"Lay your foundations with sapphires"* (Isa. 54:11). Our Husband is building us a house. This is not only the spiritual house that He is building within us, but it is also the house Jesus spoke about in John 14:2:

In My Father's house are many mansions. If it were not so, I would have told you. I go to prepare a place for you.

This is our heavenly home. I can't wait! He is laying our foundations with these precious stones. The word *foundation* "in a literal sense...can refer to laying the foundations of a building, primarily the Temple."[2] As we read in First Corinthians 6:19, *"Your body is the temple of the Holy Spirit."* He's building a pretty strong foundation in our spirits as well! Praise be to our precious Husband!

Sapphire represents "the height of celestial hope." The biblical gemstone meaning behind *sapphire* is:

> Those who are waiting with sure hope in whose life and ways the Highest is pleased. As the color of the sky, Sapphire signifies those who placed on the earth aspire for heavenly things and who despise all worldly matters just as if they were not on earth. "Our citizenship is in heaven" Philippians 3:20.[3]

Wow! I like the part about "waiting with sure hope in whose life and ways the Highest is pleased." *Baruch atah Adonai*—which is Hebrew for "Blessed are You, O Lord our God."

Rubies

Second, Isaiah lists rubies—*"I will make your pinnacles of rubies..."* (Isa. 54:12). Just what is a *pinnacle? Webster's* says it is a "high point like a spire." Imagine those great red rubies gleaming up in the sky. The meaning of rubies is listed as "preciousness, of great value, costly glories, wisdom, and prized treasure."[4] I can hear our Husband saying, "You are of great value and worth to Me; you are My most prized treasure, My love." *Baruch atah Adonai.*

Crystal

Third, Isaiah lists crystal: *"Your gates of crystal..."* (Isa. 54:12). In my research, I discovered that crystalline quartz also has the name *amethyst.* This gem is described as:

> The constant thought of the heavenly kingdom in humble souls. It signifies the heart of the lowly that died with Christ. It signifies those who pray for their enemies. Amethyst represents this virtue or virtues to pray for those who persecute you.[5]

I am humbled just thinking of what this beauty represents.

Precious Stones

Fourth, Isaiah lists precious stones: *"And all your walls of precious stones"* (Isa. 54:12). Biblical scholars believe this parallels the stones listed in the Revelation 21. These 12 layers of "precious stones" represent the foundation of the spiritual city of the New Jerusalem. (See Revelation 21:18-21.) They also represent the 12 tribes of the children of Israel. I find this stuff fascinating, so please let me indulge myself a moment! It is also believed that the 12 gems mentioned in the Book of Revelation are directly connected with each of the 12 apostles. Twelve tribes, 12 disciples—the number 12 represents, "Divine Government, apostolic fullness."[6] Could He be giving us the fullness we need in Him? Oh yes, He wants us to have it!

He's building up our spiritual walls, our gates, all around us. He is building great columns up to the sky. Our Jehovah-Jireh has even given us a foundation to stand on. That stone, that solid foundation, is Yeshua. First Peter 2:4-5 says:

> *Coming to Him as to a living stone, rejected indeed by men, but chosen by God and precious* [Jesus]*, you* [we] *also as living stones, are being built up a spiritual house, a holy priesthood, to offer up spiritual sacrifices acceptable to God through Jesus Christ.*

We are a holy priesthood—called to be "holy priests" to the Most High!

Reading on in First Peter, we find,

> *But you are a chosen generation, a royal priesthood, a holy nation, His own special people, that you may proclaim the praises of Him who called you out of darkness into His marvelous light;…now the people of God, who had not obtained mercy but now have obtained mercy* (1 Peter 2:9-10).

We are His royal priesthood. He has chosen *us,* and *we* are special to our Husband Redeemer. We see here again the word *mercy,* which parallels what I wrote in the last chapter about Hosea 2:23, *"I will have mercy on her who had not obtained mercy...." We* have obtained mercy through Him, the one who rent the veil, our own Savior Redeemer, Yeshua. Hallelujah!

Healing Scriptures

Earlier I mentioned the three keys that my friend Sonja gave me that helped me step into my healing. Here are more specific instructions for those as well as the full list of Scriptures that she gave me to pray through. I am confident that if you use these steps that God will also release healing in your life!

1. Pray the Scriptures three times a day.

Start with a personalized version of Psalm 55. Also pray through the list of personalized Scriptures following this. Blanks have been added to help you personalize the Word to your life. Put in your name, your children's names, and so forth.

I listed all of my ailments at the top of the paper with all the Scriptures on it, and then I named them every morning before praying through the Scriptures. When I prayed the Scriptures at noon and night, I just referred to "my list" without naming the sicknesses every single time.

If you feel led to add other healing Scriptures, do it! Ask the precious Holy Spirit which Scriptures to add.

2. See *The Passion of the Christ,* even if you've already seen it.

3. Take daily communion.

I took communion with actual red wine and unleavened bread or crackers. Of course, you may take it with grape juice and bread if you like. It is the thought and act that counts. I personally wanted to imitate as closely as possible what Yeshua and His disciples did. The Lord's Supper was instituted in the following chapters: Matthew 26:26-29, Mark 14:22-25, Luke 22:19-20, and First Corinthians 11:23-26.

You may feel led to fast if you can. Jesus said, *"However, this kind does not go out except by prayer and fasting"* (Matt. 17:21). However, if you're like me and too ill to fast, it is not required. Instead, fast a daily ritual or routine—especially something that gets in the way of time with your precious Husband Healer.

As for me, I will call upon God, and the Lord will save me [add names of children or others here] [from _____]. *Evening, morning and at noon will I utter my complaint and moan and sigh, and* **He will hear my voice.** *He has redeemed my life in peace from the battle* [of _____] *that was against me [so that none came near me], for they were many who strove with me* (Psalm 55:16-18 AMP).

Your right hand, O Lord, is glorious in power; Your right hand, O Lord, shatters the enemy [of _____] (Exodus 15:6 AMP).

He delivers the afflicted in their affliction [of _____] *and opens their ears [to His voice] in* [their] *adversity* [of _____] (Job 36:15 AMP).

...By the Word of your lips, I have avoided the ways of the violent [including _____] *(the paths of the destroyer)* (Psalm 17:4 AMP).

My eyes are ever toward the Lord, for He will pluck my feet out of the net [of _____] (Psalm 25:15 AMP).

[Lord,] turn to me and be gracious to me, for I am lonely and afflicted [by _____] (Psalm 25:16 AMP).

O keep me, Lord, and deliver me [from _____], *let me not be ashamed or disappointed, for my trust and my refuge are in You* (Psalm 25:20 AMP).

The Lord is my strength and my [impenetrable] Shield; my heart trusts in, relies on, and confidently leans on Him, and I am helped [in this _____]... (Psalm 28:7 AMP).

Many evils confront the [consistently] righteous; but the Lord delivers him out of them all (Psalm 34:19 AMP).

Psalm 91 (It's too long to quote it all here, but pray this whole Psalm.)

Then they cried to the Lord in their trouble [of _____], *and He delivered them out of their distresses* [of _____] (Psalm 107:6 AMP).

He sends forth His word and heals them and rescues them from the pit and destruction [of _____] (Psalm 107:20 AMP).

I mount up to heaven, and I go down again to the depths; my courage is melted because of my plight. I reel to and fro like a drunk man and am at my wits end. All my wisdom has come to nothing. Then, I called out to the Lord, in my desperate condition and He brought me out of my distress. He calms the storm to a gentle whisper, so that the waves are still. Then I am glad, and He brings me to my desired haven (Psalm 107:26-30, paraphrase).

Save my life, O Lord, for Your name's sake: in Your righteousness, bring my life out of trouble and free me from the distress [of _____] (Psalm 143:11 AMP).

Stretch forth Your hand from above; rescue me and deliver me out of these great waters, and from the hands of hostile [_____]... (Psalm 144:7 AMP).

The [uncompromisingly] righteous is delivered out of trouble [of _____], *and the wicked gets into it instead* (Proverbs 11:8 AMP).

O Lord, be gracious to us; we have waited [expectantly] for You. Be the arm [of your servants—their strength and defense] every morning, our salvation in the time of trouble [in _____] (Isaiah 33:2 AMP).

I, your God have a firm grip on you and I'm not letting go. I'm telling you "Don't panic. I am right here to help you [in _____]" (Isaiah 41:13, paraphrase).

I will deliver over you out of the hands of the wicked, and I will redeem you out of the palms of the terrible and ruthless tyrants [named _____] (Jeremiah 15:21 AMP).

And whoever shall call on the name of the Lord shall be delivered and saved [from _____]... (Joel 2:32 AMP).

You will know [experience for yourself] *the Truth, and the Truth will set you free* [from _____] (John 8:32 AMP).

So if the Son liberates you [makes you free... from] [_____], *you are really and unquestionably free* (John 8:36 AMP).

And the peace of God, which passes all understanding, will guard your hearts and minds through Christ Jesus (Philippians 4:7).

PRAYER NUGGET

Our most precious and heavenly Father, help us this day as You have called us as a holy priesthood. Even as Yeshua, the living stone, was rejected, so too, Lord, are we. But help us to know, Father, that You, O Lord, are building up our spiritual homes, that royal priesthood through our precious Lord and Savior.

Oh Father, helps us to bring our complaints to You as it says in Psalm 55. In our affliction, You are there, for Your strength is made perfect in our weakness. Thank You for Your healing stripes, for You were wounded for our transgressions, You were bruised for our iniquities, and by Your stripes, Yeshua, we are healed!

You love us so much Father! It is an everlasting love that we cannot even begin to grasp—a love that reaches down into the depths of our souls and pulls us out of hell itself. Thank You for Your great grace, Your marvelous grace toward us, the grace that pardons our sins even when we don't deserve it. I receive Your grace, Your mercy toward me this day, Father. I love You, my precious Lord and Savior. Thank You for all You've done, and thank You for enduring the cross for me! Amen!

ENDNOTES

1. Darlene Bishop; http://www.darlenebishop.org.

2. *The Hebrew-Greek Key Word Study Bible KJV* (Chattanooga, TN: AMG Publishers, 2008), commentary on Isaiah 54:11.

3. Paul Phelps, "The Jewel Stones of Israel's Twelve Tribes"; http://www.eifiles.cn/js-en.htm; accessed December 1, 2011.

4. "Gemstone Meanings," *Cross of Light Diamond;* http://www.coldiamond.com/Gemstone-meanings.html; accessed August 11, 2011.

5. "Everything About Gemstones and Jewelry"; http://www.jewelinfo4u.com; accessed August 11, 2011.

6. "Symbolism in the Bible," *Christ Centered Mall Teaching;* http://www.christcenteredmall.com/teachings/symbolism/numbers.htm; accessed August 11, 2011.

PERSONAL
Notes

_____

_____

_____

_____

_____

_____

_____

_____

_____

_____

_____

_____

_____

_____

_____

_____

_____

_____

_____

_____

_____

_____

_____

_____

_____

_____

_____

Chapter Six

HIS PEACE; HIS RIGHTEOUSNESS

All your children shall be taught by the Lord, and great shall be the peace of your children (Isaiah 54:13).

Children—the most beautiful, precious gifts of all. As it says in the Psalms, *"Happy is the man who has his quiver is full of them..."* (Ps. 127:5).

Yet many of us have spent countless nights on our knees, even on our faces, before Jehovah pleading for Him to watch over our drug-addicted daughter, our alcoholic son, our grandson who has turned to a life of crime, our niece whose mind has gone into darkness—a depression so deep that we wonder if she'll ever find her way out.

I had a time in my life when both children decided to move back to their dad's. My daughter was only 12 at the time. This was no small move; their father lived 400 miles away. Without going into all the details, I'm sure you can imagine the heart-struggle here. I was starting to get ill (as I mentioned in Chapter 5), and I really didn't have the strength to fight.

PRAYING FOR OUR KIDS

However, over the course of the next few months, as I spent much time on my face before our heavenly Father, praying for my children. I found many Scriptures speaking about my children, which I have listed below for those who may be in a similar situation. Our Husband Redeemer feels our broken hearts. He knows our pain when our children are gone, no matter the reason.

As I prayed and opened up His Word at that particular time, I received this from Jeremiah 31:15-17:

> *Thus says the Lord: "A voice was heard in Ramah, lamentation and bitter weeping, Rachel* [put in your name here] *weeping for her children, refusing to be comforted for her children, because they are no more." Thus says the Lord: "Refrain your voice from weeping, and your eyes from tears; for your work shall be rewarded, says the Lord, and they shall come back from the land of the enemy. There is hope in your future," says the Lord, "That your children shall come back to their own border."*

Just as Isaiah was sent on a mission to Israel, Jeremiah was sent approximately 50 years later. As I prayed this over my children, it gave me great comfort. God continued to provide more *rhema* Words for my situation, many from Jeremiah:

> *For thus says the Lord: "Just as I have brought all this great calamity on this people* [perhaps He's correcting us, testing us, or stretching us] *so I will bring on them all the good that I have promised them....I will cause their captives to return," says the Lord* (Jeremiah 32:42,44).

> *Call to Me, and I will answer you, and show you great and mighty things, which you do not know* (Jeremiah 33:3).

> *Behold, I will bring it health and healing; I will heal them and reveal to them the abundance of peace and truth. And I will cause the captives of Judah and the captives of Israel to return, and will build those places as at the first* (Jeremiah 33:6-7).

> *"The voice of joy and the voice of gladness, the voice of the bridegroom and the voice of the bride, the voice of those who will say: 'Praise the Lord of hosts, for the Lord is good, for His mercy endures forever'—and of those who will bring the sacrifice of praise into the house of the Lord. For I will cause the captives of the land to return as at the first," says the Lord* (Jeremiah 33:11).

I had to include all of that one—isn't it awesome! The Bride (us), the Bridegroom (Him), mercy, praise, captives returning—wow! It's another heavenly kiss!

"Behold, the days are coming," says the Lord, "that I will perform that good thing which I have promised to the house of Israel and to the house of Judah" (Jeremiah 33:14).

I got so many Scriptures that I did what it says in Habakkuk 2:2— *"Write the vision and make it plain on tablets, that he may run who reads it."* I hung those love notes from Abba Father up on a wall in my bedroom. Have they all come to pass? Some have, and some haven't. But as it says in Habakkuk 2:3:

For the vision is yet for an appointed time, but at the end it will speak, and it will not lie, though it tarries, wait for it...

We must write these and other Words the Lord speaks to us on our "tablet," holding fast and firm to them. It may not always turn out as we would like, perhaps because of timing or some other reason, but the hope in and through those words will get us through.

Abba Will Preserve Them

My son did come back home after a year, and it seemed there was anything but peace. He was struggling, and so was I. I had just had my healing from the Lord a few months earlier, but then had a car wreck, and I definitely was not up to full-speed yet. Suddenly, I found an angry young man in my household. This was during his teen years, the years in high school that are hard for so many. We teachers see our fair share of this, especially for those teens out of broken or abusive homes. Trouble can rear its ugly head in any home at any time.

I was praying and interceding for my son one particular day; I was just about at my wit's end. A few months before, I had attended a church service about an hour's drive away. They were hosting the pastors from Jesus Calls Ministries from India. I picked up a monthly magazine that this ministry publishes and read it within that week. I then laid it down by my other books.

So as I was walking and praying and really putting it out before our Father, saying things like, "Please help my son in this backslidden condition," "Please don't forget him," and so on, my eyes glanced over at this magazine lying off to the side. It was flipped open to a page that had these Scriptures in bold: *"Leave your fatherless children; I will preserve them alive..."* (Jer. 49:11) and *"I will heal their backsliding; I will love them freely..."* (Hos. 14:4). I quickly received peace once reading these precious Words—more love letters from our Husband to us. Things truly started to settle down after that. Praise the Lord!

FIGHTING FOR MY DAUGHTER

Soon after that, I knew I had been given strength again, and it was time to bring my daughter back. This was going to be a fight, and it did not turn out as planned. I felt led by the Lord, yet I ended up losing her in a court battle. I was not doing things I shouldn't have been. I was a good mom, yet I still had her taken away. The devil comes to steal, kill, and destroy (see John 10:10), and he had done it.

The children first left at the start of my illness, and even I didn't know how sick I was at that point. After my healing and as I gained my strength back, I felt able to take back what devil had stolen, but it was too late. I remember singing a song to my daughter when she was a baby, "You are my sunshine, my only sunshine. You make me happy when skies are grey. You'll never know, dear, how much I love you. Please don't take my sunshine away." That song summarizes how I felt when she moved away and when I eventually lost custody of her; my sunshine had been taken away.

To make matters worse, I knew why it had happened. I had been married to someone who often told me, "I will destroy you before you get divorced from me" or "I will destroy you before you can get the kids out of state." I also knew that the liberal visitation schedule we had worked out for the children when I had custody would not be honored once he had them. Now that the tables were turned, I knew he would suddenly "have trouble" getting them to me. This had already played out in a small way when he had both children (before getting full custody of our daughter). Before, if they got out of school on a Wednesday and then were out for a full week, I used to take them to him that night right after school. But once he had our children, he wouldn't bring them to me until the week-end—cutting into our precious time together. I knew it was not going to be a good thing once he had full control of our daughter.

A precious brother in the Lord stayed on the phone with me for what seemed like most of the night after I lost custody. If it hadn't been for Brother David and the knowledge that I still had a son to raise, I probably would have ended it. I couldn't read the Word or even talk to Father for over a day. When I finally did, I was like, *Why Lord...what happened?*

THE LORD ANSWERS

Sometimes God shows us hard things, and here is the hard thing He showed me. I opened to Psalm 44:

But You have cast us off and put us to shame, and You do not go out with our armies. You make us turn back from the enemy, and those who hate us have taken spoil for themselves. You have given us up like sheep intended for food and have scattered us among the nations...

All this has come upon us, but we have not forgotten You, nor have we dealt falsely with Your covenant. Our heart has not turned back, nor have our steps departed from Your way; but You have severely broken us...

If we had forgotten the name of our God, or stretched out our hands to a foreign god, would not God search this out? For He know the secrets of the heart. Yet for Your sake we are killed all day long; we are accounted as sheep for the slaughter. Awake! Why do You sleep, O Lord? Arise! Do not cast us off forever. Why do You hide Your face, and forget our affliction and our oppression? For our soul is bowed down to the dust; our body clings to the ground. Arise for our help, and redeem us for Your mercies' sake (Psalm 44:9-11;17-19;20-26).

This was a hard thing, but I like the Psalmist's plea to the Lord in the last sentence as he looked for Him to arise for "our redemption and mercies' sake." Months later, as I was continuing to seek the Father about what had happened, He gave me a Scripture out of Psalm 60:

You have shown Your people hard things.... Is it not You, O God, who cast us off? And You, O God who did not go out with our armies? Give us help from trouble, for the help of man is useless. Through God we will do valiantly, for it is He who shall tread down our enemies (Psalm 60:3,10-12).

It is going to be through Him and in His timing that we succeed. Our lives and purposes are in His control.

THE PEACE OF YOUR CHILDREN

I went to church that Sunday after losing custody, and a friend of mine, Chris, who did not know what was going on, told me she had seen a vision of me a few days before. She then called a mutual friend in our church because she had seen me in great distress. This friend told her that I was away in a custody battle. So as I was up in the choir just a few days after court, trying to hold it together as best I could, Chris started giving me Scriptures out of Isaiah 54:

O you afflicted one, tossed with tempest, and not comforted. Behold, I will lay your stones with colorful gems...and all your walls of precious stones. All your children shall be taught by the Lord, and great shall be the peace of your children (Isaiah 54:11-13).

Chris recently jogged my memory on this. As soon as she quoted, *"And great shall be the peace of your children,"* I remembered her saying that at church that day. I remember thinking that Father was going to take care of my children even if I wasn't allowed to. Oh dear ones, I **know** what it's like to have children taken away through no fault of your own. I also know that as I started to refocus on my Maker, my Husband, He started to tell me, "It's OK; your children are OK; you are OK. There will be peace."

In writing this chapter, I started pondering Psalm 44 even more, wondering, "Have I missed something all those years, Father?" I picked up the Tanach to see it written in a different light. What stood out right away was the heading that preceded this chapter in the Psalms: "Vividly portraying the recurring oppressions and persecutions of exile, Israel pleads for strength to endure until it is redeemed."[1] Israel understood persecution and oppression; they knew to pray for strength. This is a very good lesson for us. Let us pray for strength to endure until the time of our redemption comes. Amen!

EXCEEDINGLY ABUNDANTLY BEYOND

A few years later, my son and I went through Round Two. I'm sure many can relate. I remember talking to someone about this, and she made the comment, "Sons have a hard time growing up sometimes, as I've seen this with my husband's boys." Have you ever noticed, when the drama first starts, it seems like there is no way out?

I attended a church service out of town, and I gave a testimony about what my son and I were going through. Several people came up after the service and gave me prayers and encouragement. As I was getting ready to leave, one dear brother in the Lord timidly came up and asked if he could give me some Scriptures. I was like, "Well, of course!"

He shared that at one time, both of his sons were not saved. He told me he was out of town one weekend, and he "happened" to attend a service where a well-known minister was preaching. The pastor "happened" to be doing a teaching from Ephesians about how to pray the Scriptures to get your loved ones saved.

I said, "Wait a minute; my son is already saved."

He said, "No matter, this is good to pray over anyone. I even pray the prayers over myself." Then he added, "I prayed this over my sons, and within two to three weeks, both of them were saved!"

I excitedly said, "Show me what you got," as I knew this revelation could be life-changing for me and the many others I would share it with.

As he was opening up his Bible, he said, "It's Ephesians 1:16-21 and also Ephesians 3:14-21." I was opening my Bible at the same time so I could mark the verses. He then said, "In the place of 'you,' put in your children's names, lost loved ones' names, whoever the Lord lays on your heart, and pray those Scriptures over them." He continued, "For instance, here in Ephesians 1:16 it says:

> *I do not cease to give thanks for you....* [here put in your son's name, your daughter, your uncle, your friends, whoever], *making mention of you in my prayers: that the God of our Lord Jesus Christ, the Father of glory, may give to you the spirit of wisdom and revelation in the knowledge of Him, the eyes of your understanding being enlightened; that you* [enter names here again if you'd like] *may know what is the hope of His calling, what are the riches of the glory of His inheritance in the saints, and what is the exceeding greatness of His power toward us who believe, according to the working of His mighty power which He worked in Christ when He raised Him from the dead and seated Him at His right hand in the heavenly places, far above all principality and power and might and dominion, and every name that is named, not only in this age but also in that which is to come* (Ephesians 1:16-21)."

Then he continued, "And over here in chapter 3, start at verse 14, where it says:

For this reason I bow my knees to the Father of our Lord Jesus Christ, from whom the whole family in heaven and earth is named, that He would grant you [add the names of those you're praying for] *according to the riches of His glory, to be strengthened with might through His Spirit in the inner man, that Christ may dwell in your hearts through faith; that you, being rooted and grounded in love, may be able to comprehend with all the saints what is the width and length and depth and height—to know the love of Christ which passes knowledge; that you may be filled with all the fullness of God. Now to Him who is able to do exceedingly abundantly above all that we ask or think, according to the power that works in us, to Him be glory in the church by Christ Jesus to all generations, forever and ever. Amen* (Ephesians 3:14-21)."

Wow! I can just feel the power erupting out of those living, breathing *rhema* Words from the Lord. God's Holy Scripture is His Word, full of His promises to us. What a powerful teaching, and what a powerful way to pray over our children, our loved ones!

The word *power* is used five times in Ephesians chapters 1 and 3. *Power* comes from the Greek word *dunamis,* which means "specifically miraculous power (usually by implication, a miracle itself)...ability, strength, force."[2] Obviously, it is where we get our English word *dynamite* from.

However, in Ephesians 1:21 and 3:10, it speaks of *"principalities and powers."* This use of the word *power* comes from the Greek word *exousia,* which "denotes the executive power...delegated influence," as in "power over persons, things, dominion, authority, rule."[3] Father God has given us that rulership, that authority to pray over our loved ones. It is authority of "license, liberty, free choice."[4] It's like our heavenly Father says, "Here, look at what I've given you. Send your prayers up to Me over your children, your loved ones. I've given you the license to do it; there is liberty (freedom) for their souls if you do."

DON'T LOSE HEART

Don't wimp out on praying for your children, your loved ones, and even those you don't know, dear hearts. Yours may be the only prayers going up to Heaven on their behalf. The Word says, *"Believe on the Lord Jesus Christ, and you will be saved, you and your household"* (Acts 16:31). Claim it over *your* household. What an honor and a privilege it is to pray for His precious lost loved ones, His precious lost souls. There is *power* in those words that you pray and speak over them. Father God listens and acts; He is not through yet! Fight for their spiritual, emotional, and physical well-being, as well as the calling that Abba Father has placed upon their lives.

I had an experience recently talking with a friend. I asked her if she had heard anything from the young son of her brother-in-law. He had gone to live with his mother over four states away. She said, "No, nothing. He is a lost cause anyway."

I said, *"No!* He's not a lost cause! Keep praying for him; *keep* praying for him."

It took me by surprise when she said that. I don't believe our heavenly Father ever sees any of us as a lost cause while we are still living and breathing on this earth! Jesus tells us in Luke 18:1, *"Men always ought to pray and not lose heart...."* We must not lose heart, dear ones!

I love the parable of the lost sheep (see Matt. 18:10-14). The above incident reminds me of it. Our heavenly Father is searching for that one lost one. If it's you, He's looking for you. If it's your child, your nephew, your friend's daughter, He's looking for that lost child. Oh, He knows where the lost one is, but He is waiting. I truly believe He is waiting on prayers from His people for that soul. *"Even so it is not the will of your Father who is in heaven that one of these little ones should perish"* (Matt. 18:14). Abba Father and the heavenly angels rejoice when one comes to Him. I can just see a heavenly party complete with dancing and singing on those streets of gold!

STOLEN PEACE

As I work in the school system, I continue to ponder the meaning of *"And great shall be the peace of your children."* What steals our children's peace? It's the same things that steal ours. Bottom line: Peace is stolen when we start to get out of line with the Father's Word. Of course, the majority of children aren't even churched anymore. Our kids are dealing with cultural forces tearing at their hearts, their minds, and their very souls.

One of the biggest stealers of our children's peace is teen pregnancy. I saw a commercial for a documentary TV show that ran recently. It was about teen sex and pregnancy, and they showed a young girl crying, speaking of her and her boyfriend, saying, "Everything has changed for me, but nothing has changed for him." I'm amazed as I hear teens—especially young girls—talk about it and even try to convince others to have babies if they have already had one. It's almost normal, it seems; we've all become so complacent to it.

Yet studies show that the rates of poverty and other ills that come with it are rampant among teen mothers.[5] I know how hard it was to end up divorced and then raising children as a single parent. I was in my early 30s, and it was so difficult then. I can't imagine having all that responsibility when so young. As parents, we must keep talking to our children about this. Even when it seems they don't listen, we must not give up!

Dear hearts, I know the worries about this. I am still holding my breath over it myself since I have older children who are barely out of high school. Still, no matter what happens, I know Father God can work everything for good for those who love the Lord (see Rom. 8:28), and babies are born into single-parent households every day. I admire those who raise their babies, as well as those who have the strength to choose adoption (I am adopted, after all).

A friend of mine had a dream about teens having babies, some would say "babies having babies." In the dream, she saw high school–age kids.

The girls were pushing each other to get pregnant. (I have actually seen this in the real world too.) She felt as if they were trying to pass that spirit around, as if provoking one another. They were talking about planting pumpkin seeds (which in the dream meant "getting pregnant"). As soon as a young girl would get pregnant, she would sit outside the school next to her pumpkin plant looking sad.

There was one girl, however, who refused to be corrupted by the others. She then ran across some boys who tried to get her attention by throwing a basketball net at her. But a glass wall was protecting her, and she didn't even pay attention to the boys. My friend said it felt as if she had some special protection around her.

This is profound! We all have this special protection around us, like the girl in the dream, if we choose to stay away from sin and to live in obedience. It is so simple, yet so many of us don't do it! All we need to do is stay on track with God and cut out the foolishness; then the drama will disappear. But it's like we are addicted to the stuff that brings the drama. Are we addicted to drama, then? It sounds kind of crazy, but it seems to describe most of the human race from the time of the Israelites on.

WALK IN THE SPIRIT

We discussed previously the importance of obedience. Here are some more treasures from God's Word about what obedience to His Word brings.

> *Walk in the Spirit, and you shall not fulfill the lust of the flesh. For the flesh lusts against the Spirit, and the Spirit against the flesh; and these are contrary to one another, so that you do not do the things you wish* (Galatians 5:16-17).

Look at Romans 7:15. I identify with Paul when he says, *"For what I am doing, I do not understand. For what I will to do, that I do not practice; but what I hate, that I do."* Many of us know what to do but are just not doing it. We're sounding a little like Paul. Well, what then?

Read Galatians 5:19-21, which lists the works of the flesh and their result:

Adultery, fornication, uncleanness, lewdness, idolatry, sorcery, hatred, contentions, jealousies, outbursts of wrath, selfish ambitions...envy, murders, drunkenness...and the like...those who practice such things will not inherit the kingdom of God.

Think about the girl in the dream who refuses to get caught up in the lies of the world. What would happen if we also refused to get caught up in the lies? Continuing on, Galatians 5:22-26 says:

But the fruit of the Spirit is love, joy, peace, longsuffering, kindness, goodness, faithfulness, gentleness, self-control...those who are Christ's have crucified the flesh with its passions and desires... Let us not become conceited, provoking one another...

I want this fruit for me and my children and for those around me. Patience, love, kindness, selflessness—these are true jewels, true treasures.

THE DATING ISSUE

So many of my friends and I are leading the single life right now. Many single moms and dads like myself must also deal with the dating issue. One of my best friends just went through two engagements in less than a year. I recently went over to talk with her, and the thing she was most upset with was what those breakups had done to her children. Her children's peace had been removed through her admittedly bad choices. Even though her decision to break up was admirable, she confessed to me, "I had been looking at those relationships to make me whole, and we know that never works."

She's right; it doesn't. She reflected further, "You know, when I told my 8-year-old that I wasn't getting married, he stuck his head in his coat and cried for over an hour, saying, 'I thought I was gonna get a step-dad.'" She said she made herself stay with him through it all. "I wanted to feel his pain of what I had done to him through my bad choices. I needed to feel it. Here I am running around, not really searching out God in these major decisions—yet all the way saying, 'It's in God's will.' Then in the meanwhile, I'm devastating those closest to me."

I have seen that time and time again; it's almost as if we use God as an excuse. We say, "It's His will" and then flip when things are not working and say, "Oh, it's not in His will." Did God change His mind that quickly, or are our own selfish desires coming into play here? All in all, many people get hurt, and I don't think that's God's will.

STATISTICS ABOUT SEX

Connected to the issue of being single and dating is the topic of premarital sex. In doing some research, I was shocked at what I found related to premarital sex, not only with our teens, but in the single parent age group as well. According to research done by the Barna Group, here are some statistics from adults who consider themselves born-again. Thirty-five percent believe it is "morally acceptable" to have premarital sex. Another 49 percent of these adults feel it is "morally acceptable" behavior to live with someone before marriage! Researchers believe that "morality is likely to decline further."[6] The article did not state the ages of the adult "born-agains"; however, it did point out that the older people are, the less likely they are to buy into morally unacceptable behavior. Whatever the case, these statistics reveal a huge problem that is growing.

In these endtimes, our sex-charged culture is fueled by easy access to pornographic material on the Internet and television. Many good people are in a battle. I have a close Christian friend who has a terrible gambling addiction. She has amazing insight from the Lord, yet satan uses the lure of a money "quick-fix" to keep her straying. We must not judge; we all have our weaknesses. Until we walk in other people's shoes, we'll never know what they've been through. I do know that when this friend was young, she went through more in a few years' time than most go through in a lifetime. Dear hearts, we have to remember our Husband has more for us than the world has to offer. Fill up with Him! He offers us freedom from all and any addiction and we *can* live righteously through Him!

Looking at the stats, it is no wonder that good people are struggling, and it is no wonder that the world doesn't want anything to do with Christianity. We are supposed to *"have the mind of Christ"* (1 Cor. 2:16), yet it seems the Bride, His Church, has anything but! Sadly, many have adopted a *world-view* instead of Christ's view. We need to return to our first love! Revelation 2:4 admonishes, *"Nevertheless, I have somewhat against thee, because thou hast left thy first love"* (KJV). We must return to our Husband, return to our first love. Let's fall in love with Yeshua again—how sweet and precious He is!

Battling Jezebel

So what's the point? If you or others you know are wrestling with premarital sex, lust, and all that goes with it, it's time to look again at Ephesians 6:12:

> *For we do not wrestle against flesh and blood, but against principalities, against powers, against rulers of the darkness of this age, against spiritual hosts of wickedness in the heavenly places.*

Many people who struggle with these issues are actually wrestling against a seducing spirit that has its roots in Jezebel. For the guys, I've heard a pastor call it the "Jeze-billy spirit." The story of Jezebel is located in First and Second Kings.

Yeshua alerted the Church in Revelation 2 against the spirit of Jezebel, which can lead God's own people into sexual immorality and idol worship. This spirit also loves to control and manipulate. Most times we don't even realize when we are under its influence. For example, the world tells us to dress a certain way and act a certain way. Too quickly, it becomes the accepted norm among many Christians because of the manipulation of the world system, but it doesn't make it right. We must beware and ask

Father to show us where we need to clean up our act. Let's get real about this so we can heal and then use our victory to be able to help others.

This is serious business, brothers and sisters. I pray the Holy Spirit starts to convict your hearts. *"For the wages of sin is death..."* (Rom. 6:23). It might be a spiritual death or a physical death. Whatever it is, it's time to repent. First Corinthians 6:18-20 says:

> *Flee sexual immorality. Every sin that a man does is outside the body, but he who commits sexual immorality sins against his own body. Or do you not know that your body is the temple of the Holy Spirit who is in you...and you are not your own? For you were bought with a price; therefore glorify God in your body and in your spirit, which are God's.*

If you continue in this sin—any sin—be mindful of this verse in Romans 1:28—*"And even as they did not like to retain God in their knowledge, God gave them over to a reprobate mind..."* (KJV). The Greek word for *reprobate* is *adokimos,* which means "...rejected, worthless (literal and moral)...castaway."[7] We have all seen people like this, who are so caught up in sins that they just don't think rightly anymore.

Our heavenly Father knows we cannot fight this evil spirit (or any evil spirit) in our own selves. Our Defender hasn't left us to fight it alone. I've heard my pastor argue that people who are Christians cannot have these types of spirits living in them. We are washed clean by the blood of the Lamb! However, Christians can get seduced and oppressed by these spirits, even (and especially) Christians who have high callings on their lives. Many people in ministry have fallen because satan went after a weakness that they had not found freedom from.

We must start praying for ourselves and for others for self-control. This is one of the fruits of the Spirit listed in Galatians 5:22. When we start to get close to the edge, Galatians 5:1 tells us:

Stand fast therefore in the liberty by which Christ has made us free, and do not be entangled again with a yoke of bondage.

We must turn around and refuse to go back into Egypt, children of the Most High! I speak from experience here and know of the battles that come with this issue. Stop here and read Galatians 5.

PASSION FOR PURITY PLAN

Satan *is* going to lie to you. It's his job. As you try to live a life of abstinence and purity, you might hear, "Well, everybody's doing it anyway," or "Don't you want to try it to make sure everything works?" How about this one: "There must be something wrong with you if you do not want to do it." You will hear these lies from many places—television, movies, your own friends, or maybe even a Christian date.

Let's face it, statistics show that most people are "doing it," both in the secular world and sadly even the Christian one. However, many know others who are wholly committed to living a life of purity before marriage. But how is it done, especially for the divorced or widowed person? How is it done in this culture?

Recently I armed myself with some articles about purity that I keep in my Bible. Keep yourself prepared, and also hand out helpful materials to friends who are struggling. Even hand your date a copy of your standards of purity so you are both on the same page. Following is my plan for purity, which I have also included in the Appendix at the end of the book. This can be copied and handed out to friends who need guidance on this subject.

1. Refuse Unequal Yoking

As Christians we are not to be "unequally yoked" (see 2 Cor. 6:14). Otherwise, you will have a battle from the start. Many believers think they can "win them over," but what usually happens is that the unbeliever "wins" as the Christian walks away from Christ.

2. Be Friends First

It is *great* to be friends first! Remember, you are brothers and sisters in the Lord. Treat each other as such! You will actually get to know one another better without the emotional and physical involvement.

3. Set Physical Boundaries

If you find, after dating as friends, that you are both marriage material and that the relationship is becoming serious, continue to keep it friendly. Set boundaries for your physical relationship. For most (probably all) people, kissing leads to other things. A lot of you are probably thinking, *Oh come on; it's just a kiss.* A kiss is not going to send you to hell, but if you start pushing the line, you're going to feel like you're there! If you find you *are* pushing that line but not going "all the way," you have to ask yourself whether you are really giving your best to God. Don't buy into the lie, "We might as well do it since we're going to get married anyway."

Sticking to only hand-holding and hugging seems to be the ticket to not getting caught up in somewhere you don't want to be. Hold to those boundaries. Why is this so important? One Scripture that **always** gets to me is when Jesus says, *"If you love Me, keep My commandments"* (John 14:15). Ouch. Kind of hits you where it hurts, doesn't it?

Are you *passionately in love* with *your Savior* enough to *obey* the commandment *"You shall not commit adultery"* (Deut. 5:18)? In modern English, this means, *don't have sex outside of marriage!* Yeshua set the bar high; it was He who said that if you even look upon another with lust you have already committed adultery in your heart (see Matt. 5:28). He knows that once you start letting that lust issue enter into your heart, you are about to fall.

4. Agree on Your Standards

Many have good intentions but don't manage to follow through. Here is a key to why that the Lord gave me years ago. I was all "prayed up," yet was seeing a Christian man who was not fully committed to the "no-sex-before-marriage" rule. I prayed about it, and when I opened my Bible, I got this jewel: *"Watch and pray, lest you enter into temptation. The spirit indeed is willing, but the flesh is weak"* (Matt. 26:41). When both people in the relationships are not committed to purity, you will be pulled down. I had to break the date.

5. Set Your Mind Back on Father

So what should you do if you find yourselves already pushing that line, or worse, having gone past it? One thing that often happens with couples who begin having sex before marriage is that they stop really communicating, reading their Bibles together, and praying together. If you truly love Jesus, you'll find a way to stop. If you both truly love each other, you will find a way to stop.

The Scripture says, *"For it is better to marry than burn **with passion**"* (1 Cor. 7:9). However, rather than rushing into a marriage that may not last, I suggest that you may want to "cool it" for a while or break up altogether in order to repent and get your heart wholly focused back on your Abba Father. This will be tough, but if you love your Savior God, pray and He will help you both to make this correction. *He* is the only one who can.

LIVING RIGHTEOUSLY

Years ago, I read a book called *The Case for Christ* by Lee Strobel (a former atheist) and wrote some excerpts out of it for a Christian college class I was taking. He had interviewed D. A. Carson, who was a research professor of the New Testament at Trinity Evangelical Divinity School.

Strobel asked Dr. Carson about Christ's deity. In his answer we find that wonderful, beautiful word *grace* again. Here is a small quote from their conversation:

> Strobel observed (while Christ was on earth), "Not only did Christ forgive sin, but he asserted that he himself was without sin. And certainly sinlessness is an attribute of deity."

Dr. Carson replied, "Yes, historically in the West, people considered most holy have also been the most conscious of their own failures and sins. They are people who are aware of their shortcoming and lusts and resentments, and they're fighting them honestly by the grace of God. In fact, they're fighting them so well that others take notice and say, 'There is a holy man or woman.'"[8]

We have all seen this in people who are trying to live right and holy lives. We all have friends who have come out of the worst of the worst situations, and we see them have victory, and we have seen them struggle. It's a part of life. What sets them apart is that when they sin, when they struggle, they run back to God, back to His grace and His mercy! They stay in the fight! Running away from Him will get us nowhere. Besides, He knows where we are anyway; we can run, but we can't hide!

We cannot underestimate the importance of virtue. Second Peter 1:3-7 says:

> *Through the knowledge of Him who called us by glory and virtue, by which have been given to us exceedingly great and precious promises, that through these you may be partakers of the divine nature, having escaped the corruption that is in the world through lust. ...Giving all diligence, add to your faith virtue, to virtue knowledge, to knowledge self-control, to self-control perseverance, to perseverance godliness, to godliness brotherly kindness and to brotherly kindness love.*

Talk about a list of character builders! I want (and need!) that whole list! It goes on to say that if we lack those things, we are short-sighted:

> *He who lacks these things is short-sighted, even to blindness, and has forgotten that he was cleansed from his old sins...be even more diligent to make your call and election sure, for if you do these things you will never stumble* (2 Peter 1:9-10).

We must add virtue, dear hearts (and don't forget the rest of the list). Let's quit stumbling.

A Coming Awakening

In righteousness you shall be established... (Isaiah 54:14).

Our text in Isaiah goes on to promise that we will be established in righteousness. Just as hope is returning to the Israelites in these verses, so too I believe hope is returning to this generation, the young and old alike. Hope is returning for this lost generation of children. I know many believers who have been standing in the gap all over this nation and who have been on their faces before our most holy Father, crying out Second Chronicles 7:14:

> *If My people who are called by My name will humble themselves, and pray and seek My face, and turn from their wicked ways, then I will hear from heaven, and will forgive their sin and heal their land.*

I believe an awakening and a love outpouring by the Holy Spirit is coming soon. Many in the prophetic realm believe Father God is about to send a great awakening and outpouring to America like we've never seen. Let it be so, Lord Jesus; let it be so!

We may still be on our faces before the Lord pleading for our children and their peace. Israel may still be waiting on peace, on the Messiah (although many are accepting Yeshua and now believe)! But as we know, true peace, true shalom, will not come until our coming King returns to this earth.

If you need to make a U-turn, if you need to repent, then do it! It's better to suffer while doing what's right then to suffer for doing what's wrong (see 1 Pet. 3:17). *God allows U-turns!*

As part of the declaration that we will be established in righteousness, God gives us several promises:

> *You shall be far from oppression, for you shall not fear; and from terror, for it shall not come near you* (Isaiah 54:14).

Living rightly for Him gives us supernatural peace. Oh yes, we'll still have trials, but if we're living in righteousness for Him, guilt, fear, and terror are not in the picture anymore. Thank You, *Jehovah-Shalom!*

PRAYER NUGGET

Our most gracious and heavenly Father, I praise You and thank You for being there for us in times of earthly trials.

Even when we have felt You have left us, You still break through and give us that one ray of hope we need. We know there is only hope in You and through You, Father God. We pray for strength for us and for Israel, Father, until the time of redemption comes.

Establish us, Father, in Your righteousness and Your peace so that oppression, terror, and fear will be far from us. Father, please help those who already know You, but have somehow lost their way, to return to their first love. Forgive us, Father, and help us return back to You—our Husband, our First Love.

Establish us, Father, in virtue, knowledge, self-control, perseverance, godliness, brotherly kindness, and love. Lord, we know You desire that not one of us would be lost.

We pray, Lord, that You would grant us and our loved ones the spirit of wisdom and revelation in the knowledge of You, that the eyes of our understanding will be enlightened, and that we may know the hope of Your calling and the greatness of Your power, Father.

Strengthen us and our loved ones, Father, with might through Your Spirit in the inner person, that Christ may dwell in our hearts through faith. Root and ground us in love to know the love of Christ, which passes knowledge and fill us with all Your fullness, Father God.

Now to You, Father, who is able to do exceedingly abundantly above all that we ask or think, according to Your power that works in us—to You, Adonai, be glory in the Church by Christ Jesus forever and ever. Amen.

ENDNOTES

1. *The Stone Edition Tanach.* Brooklyn, NY: Mesorah Publications Ltd. 1996 (A Jewish Translation of the Bible), heading for Psalm 44.

2. *The Hebrew-Greek Key Word Study Bible KJV* (Chattanooga, TN: AMG Publishers, 2008), commentary on "dunamis" in Ephesians.

3. Ibid., commentary on "excousia" in Ephesians 1:21; 3:10.

4. Ibid.

5. The National Campaign to Prevent Teen and Unplanned Pregnancy, "Why it Matters: Linking Teen Pregnancy to Prevention and Other Critical Social Issues." March 2010. (www.teenpregnancy.org); accessed December 1, 2011.

6. The Barna Group, "Morality Continues to Decay," November 3, 2003; (http://www.barna.org/barna-update/article/5-barna-update/129-morality-continues-to-decay-?q=sex); accessed August 8, 2011.

7. *The Hebrew-Greek Key Word Study Bible KJV,* commentary on "adokimos" in Romans 1:28.

8. Lee Strobel, *The Case for Christ* (Grand Rapids, MI: Zondervan, 1998), 158.

PERSONAL
Notes

Chapter Seven

THE BATTLE

Indeed they shall surely assemble, but not because of Me. Whoever assembles against you shall fall for your sake (Isaiah 54:15).

I like the way the Tanach puts verse 15:

Behold, they may indeed gather together, but it is without My consent. Whoever will gather against you will fall because of you.

They shall surely assemble...they may indeed gather together—who or what is the *"they"* that is assembling (sounds like we may be getting ready to go to war) in our lives right now? Perhaps it's court dates, unpaid bills, health issues, depression, or even loneliness. Or could it be spoken and unspoken requests that have not been answered or lies and accusations? Maybe it's judgment by God's own people, those who are supposed to love us through but instead judge us through it.

All I know is, no matter what our battles are, we must press in and on and keep praying the promises. *"Whoever assembles against you shall fall for your sake."* Brave hearts, get up! Our Warrior Husband has a plan when things come against us. We may not know what it is yet, but we do know that it's satan's plan to keep us down. However, our Lord and Master says *that* plan will fall for our sakes! Keep soldiering in, keep soldiering on, brave hearts!

THE EMPTY NEST

Just recently, I got a text from my son saying, "Mom, I'm moving back to Dad's by the weekend." Later, I found out that this was not going to be the best of circumstances. A battle had presented itself. I was watching my family members put up idols in their lives, setting themselves up for lives of codependency. I have recognized this in my own life at times. I caught myself sounding like my parents, saying, "I didn't raise you this way!" The battle was in my face.

I was trying to not have a pity party, but I was grieved that both of my children would be over 400 miles away (again). I always thought we'd be close. There are too many relational dynamics here to describe. One thing I knew: I'm not done praying for my children yet. I said that with a slight smile, thinking, *OK, Father, we still have some work to do,* but also knowing that it was time for a mom to let go, to let God be in control, and to let this young man take off on his journey.

The "empty nest syndrome" that all parents go through seems to get tweaked up a notch for the single parent. Some look forward to it, but I'm not there yet. It seems to me that the single parent, the ones who become not only mom, but also dad (or vice versa), really have a *huge* adjustment at this point. This is especially true for those who haven't found that special someone yet or maybe are in the middle of a career change. Both of those were true for me. I was feeling the addition of another birthday, looking at dwindling finances, and needing to find a better job or career while everyone else just a few years older than me was already looking at retirement. I couldn't help but think, *Wait, Father, what is happening here? I'm sure many are more pulled together than I am. I feel like a failure as nothing turned out as planned. I never thought I'd be in this position!*

Of course, it's not only single people who struggle with the empty nest. I have known many married couples who threw themselves into the child-raising ring, only to find, once the children were gone, that they were now strangers to each other. It's a hard adjustment for many!

One of the reasons why we often have a hard time being ready for the next chapter of our lives is because things that we believe would come to pass have not. We find ourselves says, "Wait, Father, but You said...." I used to be one who thrived on change, but I was no longer thriving. Many have never done well with change at all. However, we have to believe that there is a purpose, especially if our change becomes a trial.

The Word says, *"They shall surely assemble...."* The battles will come. (I find it interesting I got a call just as I was starting this part of the book!) But we don't have to be overwhelmed. Though our peace may be shaken, we have a Husband who is our anchor. During all the turmoil with my children and facing the empty nest, my peace was severely tested, yet I found the comfort and strength I needed in God's promise that the trials that assemble against me will fall for my sake. He is a good Husband, and though we don't always understand why things happen (or don't happen), we can trust in His tender provision in our life!

GOING TO WAR

> *Behold, I have created the blacksmith who blows the coals in the fire, who brings forth an instrument for his work; and I have created the spoiler to destroy* (Isaiah 54:16).

This next verse in our Isaiah passage sounds like we *are* going to war. In those days, blacksmiths primarily fashioned armor and made weapons. The verse prior promises that opposition will come, but that we will overcome. *How?* We will overcome through the weapons God provides. During the Praise Mandate, I learned that praise (Judah) goes first in a spiritual battle. Praise is our weapon. As Isaiah 42:12-13 says:

> *Let them give glory to the Lord, and declare His praise in the coastlands. The Lord shall go forth like a mighty man; He shall stir up **His** zeal like a man of war, He shall cry out, yes, shout aloud; He shall prevail against His enemies.*

While we are preparing for the battle, because of our weapon of praise, *"The Lord shall go forth like a mighty man."* I love that picture! I can just see fire flashing from His eyes and hear thunder booming from his voice. I can see His intensity as He prepares to go forth and prevail against His enemies (our enemies). It's His battle anyway.

After the Praise Mandate, I was chomping at the bit to go to war, yet it was not the right time. I was praying, "Father, I'm ready to go to war. I've praised; my friends have praised. Now let's get to work and go to war" (in the Spirit, of course). But I heard nothing from Him and received no words about war. So I realized that it was the wrong time, the wrong season to go to war.

However, a few months later I was reading Isaiah 54, and when I reached verses 15-16, I started to ask, "Now, Father? Is it *now* time to war?" I got up the next day and read an Elijah List e-mail from a prophet whose prayer focuses I have followed in the past saying it was "time for war." Then another confirmation while reading the Bible—Yes, it was time for war.

I love it when I get a purpose. If you're a doer, a go-getter, you'll like this part. Don't get me wrong; spiritual warfare is definitely not fun, but it feels good to be moving with the Holy Spirit in *His* direction. James 1:22 tells us, *"But be ye doers of the Word, and not hearers only, deceiving your own selves"* (KJV). James liked "doers!" I bet James was a "doer" himself!

How We War

How do we war? Second Corinthians 10:3 says, *"Though we walk in the flesh, we do not war according to the flesh."* This is a spiritual battle, brave hearts.

It is important, as we step into battle, to make sure we're looking to God, who gives us the power, instead of the power of warfare itself. I've seen many people start "power-tripping" during warfare, saying things like, "Oh boy, I cast that ol' devil out." No matter how great our feats of spiritual war are, we must remember that we have been *given* that power. God is the source.

> *And when He had called unto **Him** His twelve disciples, He gave them power against unclean spirits, to cast them out, and to heal all manner of sickness and disease* (Matthew 10:1).

We are those disciples! However, we must make sure we're not relying in our own "self power." It's enticing to want to be back in control; we want to take on the demons, and it's great to feel like we might actually have some power. This is a trap from the enemy. However, when we are praying a heartfelt battle cry through struggle and pain, Father will remind us, "*...My grace is sufficient for thee; for My strength is made perfect in weakness...*" (2 Cor. 12:9). While being careful to avoid pride, it is OK, as we feel led by the Holy Spirit into spiritual warfare, to *relish* this time to partner with our Defender, our Shield.

When you are led into battle, you will get confirmation on it. Maybe you suddenly randomly begin turning to many Scripture verses on warfare; then your pastor preaches a message on it; then you turn on the radio and someone is talking about spiritual warfare. You get the idea. Ask the Holy Spirit for discernment. This is how you will get your specific battle plans to disarm the enemy.

What do you need to war over, brave heart? Are you wrestling with something? Do you still have words that haven't come to pass? Are your children living for the devil instead of the Lord? Do you have infirmities beyond anything you ever imagined? It's time for war!

BATTLE ARMOR

One of the most important weapons in spiritual warfare is the sword of the Spirit—our written Word from God. Every good soldier needs to put on armor.

Finally, my brethren, be strong in the Lord and in the power of His might. Put on the whole armor of God, that you may be able to stand against the wiles of the devil. **For we do not wrestle against flesh and blood, but against principalities, against powers, against the rulers of the darkness of this age, against spiritual hosts of wickedness in the heavenly places.** *Therefore take up the whole armor of God, that you may be able to withstand in the evil day, and having done all, to stand* (Ephesians 6:10-13).

The specific armor is outlined in the next passage of Ephesians:

Stand therefore, having girded your waist with the belt of truth, having put on the breastplate of righteousness, and having shod your feet with the preparation of the gospel of peace; above all, taking the shield of faith with which you will be able to quench all the fiery darts of the wicked one. And take the helmet of salvation, and the sword of the Spirit, which is the word of God; praying always with all prayer and supplication in the Spirit, being watchful to this end... (Ephesians 6:14-18).

Belt of Truth

Stand and wrap around your waist "the belt of truth." In the military, the belts that soldiers wear not only hold up their pants, but also serve as a holder for weapons. I just watched the epic movie *The Ten Commandments*, and as I read this passage, in my mind I can see Yul Brynner standing as his armor bearers strap the metal around him. *Truth* comes from the Greek word *alethia*.

> Divine truth or the faith and practice of the true religion is called "truth" either as being true in itself and derived from the true God, or as declaring the existence and will of the one true God, in opposition to the worship of false idols. Hence...to mean divine truth, gospel truth.[1]

Amen! Buckle up your "belt of truth," soldier.

Breastplate of Righteousness

What is "the breastplate of righteousness"? Putting on an armored breastplate will protect your heart, ribs, and internal organs in an earthly battle. What does it do in a spiritual one? The word *righteousness* means "of character, conduct, being just as one should be, rectitude, uprightness, virtue." The last part of the definition makes my heart jump! It reads, "Internal, where the heart is right with God, piety toward God, and hence righteousness, godliness."[2] He needs you to be spiritually right with Him so that He can help you fight and win the battle. Get your heart right, soldiers of the Most High.

Shoes of Peace

"Having shod your feet with the preparation of the gospel of peace...." Prepare yourself to walk in peace with the Word, the Gospel of our Lord. It may stir up some wrath at times from others, but be ready to be peaceful. The Scriptures say, *"A soft answer turns away wrath, but a harsh word stirs up anger"* (Prov. 15:1). That may not sound too powerful, but you're not in this war for power's sake. In God's Kingdom, you have more power when you can turn away wrath.

Shield of Faith

Pick up your *"shield of faith with which you will be able to quench all the fiery darts of the wicked one."* The shield is another piece of battle armor. Darts from the enemy are going to start flying about when you get in the battle, but all you have to do is lift your shield and have faith.

It may be easier said than done when you're in the middle of a divorce and it looks like more than your half is being taken away, or your kids are being used as leverage points, or you've lost the love of your life to another. It's easier said than done when the creditor stands knocking at your door, when you get telephone calls day and night from those looking to get paid.

But if you turn to that great faith chapter in the Bible, you'll see that God says, *"Now faith is the substance of things hoped for, the evidence of things not seen"* (Heb. 11:1). God's Word says to have faith. It also says to believe: *"For what does the Scripture say? **Abraham believed God and it was accounted to him for righteousness"*** (Rom. 4:3). Belief and righteousness wrapped up in one verse are kind of like a one-two punch.

In the last chapter I wrote about several verses in Ephesians that you should pray over your children, over your lost loved ones. It is important to remember, when you are praying (you will have nothing without earnest prayer), praying God's holy and inspired Word over them is an act of war! *You* are speaking words of hope, faith, and love over them, and satan is not going to like it; you're in a battle now!

Helmet of Salvation

Make sure you have salvation on as your helmet. A helmet protects your head—where your thoughts come from. It will protect your mind. Salvation is God's greatest gift, and it is your protection, your children's protection. Satan may win a battle, but the Lion of the tribe of Judah, Yeshua Himself, has already won the war! *"For this purpose the Son of God was manifested, that He might destroy the works of the devil"* (1 John 3:8). Hallelujah!

Sword of the Spirit

You war with the Word—your sword. You must war with truth from God's Word. Soldiers need sharp swords, piercingly sharp. When you are fighting in the Spirit, your ability to use Scripture needs to be quick and sharp. Hebrews 4:12 says, *"For the word of God is living and powerful, and sharper than any two-edged sword, piercing even to the division of soul and spirit...."* Keep studying His Holy Word, committing to memorizing some scriptural truths that speak to you. That will sharpen your sword.

WEARY IN THE FIGHT

Many of us have become weary in the battle. This is especially true when it seems to go on for months or even years. I once heard someone say, "Tears don't move God; only faith does." I'm not sure I agree with that statement about tears. Psalm 56:8-11 says:

You number my wanderings; put my tears into Your bottle: are ***they*** *not in Your book? When I cry out to You, then my enemies will turn back; this I know for God is for me. In God (I will praise His word), in the Lord (I will praise His word), in God I have put my trust; I will not be afraid. What can man do to me?*

He is a God with a heart of compassion; it's OK to tear up and cry it out, dear ones; don't hold it in. Then, ask the One who provides you strength to move you on and up from tears to trust and faith. Trust and faith will move you through the battle.

Father is looking for those who won't waver. Admittedly, I tend to be a bit of a waverer. I don't like it, but I know I am at times. It's strange, but before my mother passed away I hardly ever doubted, always knowing that *El Olam*—the Everlasting God—was working it out. Then my mother went home to be with her Savior, and when my life started to tumble after that, I seemed to stop trusting. Perhaps somewhere along the line you too have developed the wavering seed, the seed of doubt.

I like what the writer James says to do about this. He keeps it simple. Ask for wisdom in your situation. James 1:5-8 says:

If any of you lacks wisdom, let him ask of God...But let him ask in faith, with no doubting, for he who doubts is like a wave of the sea driven and tossed by the wind. For let not that man supposed that he will receive anything from the Lord; he is a double-minded man, unstable in all his ways.

I want the mountain-moving kind of faith! Father God, help us to have faith that can move mountains, even when our worlds are falling apart. When life is tough, turn on some faith music and praise the One who can give us faith to help bust through that doubt.

At the end of the armor verses in Ephesians, verse 18 says, *"Praying always with all prayer and supplication in the Spirit, being watchful to this end...."* We must pray, pray, pray, making our petitions, our requests, known to the Most High. Then we simply watch for our answers, wait for

God to act on our behalf. We must not doubt or fear or waver. I preach this one to myself. Amen!

The inspiring movie, *The Blind Side*, quotes the popular saying, "I got your back." The idea of it is comforting. It is wonderful when we are provided with spouses, family, and friends who say, "I got your back." However, we don't always get that luxury from others. Just remember, brave hearts, *God has our backs!* Others may fail us, but we don't have to depend on others! Our dependence is in God, and He is always faithful.

While writing this book, I wrecked my car after a snow storm. I wasn't hurt; however, the car was almost totaled. Just a couple months before that, I had been standing up on a stool cleaning a wall clock. While I was coming down, I missed the crosspiece on the stool and ended up falling backward onto a hardwood floor. Due to the momentum of my fall, I also slid down two steps into the sunken living room and ended up flat on my back. Thankfully, all I suffered was a bruise on the back of my arm, where it hit the stool as I was coming down.

But as I lay there counting all my pieces, I started to think, *If I'm hurt, there is no one to take care of me (ohhh poor me).* However, as I got up, I began to praise the Lord because nothing was wrong! *He* had my back. He protected me when I fell, and He protected me in the car accident. We must know that we know that we know that our heavenly Husband has our backs. I love this promise in Scripture: *"For the Lord will go before you, and the God of Israel will be your rear guard"* (Isa. 52:12).

Our Defender even gives us *angels* who have charge over us—*"In their hands they shall bear you up, lest you dash your foot against a stone"* (Ps. 91:12). Psalm 91 is a great chapter to read over and over again while in the battle. As a matter of fact, it's a great one to memorize; let's sharpen our swords! We need not give into fear when we are abandoned and alone. *He* is with us when our kids have left the nest. *He* is with us when loved ones have left. *He* is with us in every sickness. *He* has our front. *He* has our back. *He* is with us!

No Weapon...

No weapon formed against you shall prosper, and every tongue which rises against you in judgment you shall condemn... (Isaiah 54:17).

Notice the first sentence of verse 17, *"No weapon formed against you shall prosper."* A dear brother in the Lord has always pointed out this verse to me in a special way. In his unique southern drawl, he would say, "Mary, you know that verse 'no weapon formed against you shall prosper'?"

"Yes, Brother David, I do."

"Well, that means they're gonna form, but you ain't gotta worry about 'em. They're not going to prosper."

This is like several verses back where it says, *"They shall surely assemble"* (Isa. 54:15), which is followed by the promise that the assembled ones shall fall. Here, instead of *they,* it's now *weapons* that are forming, yet we are promised that these weapons will not prosper.

It is always a spiritual battle. I can see satan and his minions sharpening their swords and battle axes. "Let's see if we can bring 'em down with disease. Let's see if we can have someone hit 'em with a lawsuit. Let's see if we can have a lying tongue make them lose their job." Yet God says, *"Every tongue which rises against you in judgment you shall condemn."*

At times we lose jobs, lose friends, have lies told about us, and so forth—of course! We live in this fleshy world. Many are probably suffering right now due to the issues of life. Many more are probably suffering right now trying to live Christian lives. We are targets; that's why weapons are forming. When these things happen, we must respond by looking to Him! Many of us have been made fun of for trying to live Christian lives, even persecuted for our beliefs. Wagging tongues have not given us any rest or peace. Keep your mind stayed on Him, for He will keep you in perfect peace (see Isa. 26:3).

During a setback with a loved one, I called up a friend, telling her, "They've done nothing but make fun of me for trying to live for the Lord."

My prayer warrior friend, Pam, rose up and said, "Stop! I'm not going to let you beat yourself up anymore. Look up any Scripture you can find on suffering, trials, and testing."

I did. And something powerful happened. In filling myself with the Word, that weapon that was forming against me, which was going to be depression, isolation, and loneliness, didn't prosper. That's how we condemn those tongues that rise up against us. We don't let them prosper in the first place; we don't let satan get the upper hand. Rather, we resist him with the Word of God's truth. First Peter 5:8-9 reminds us:

> *Be sober, be vigilant because your adversary the devil walks about like a roaring lion, seeking whom he may devour. Resist him, steadfast in the faith, knowing that the same sufferings are experienced by your brotherhood in the world.*

It helps also to remember that what we go through is nothing compared to what our persecuted brothers and sisters suffer in North Korea, Saudi Arabia, and many other places around the world.

A few years ago, I typed up a story for a Christian brother who had gone to China to distribute Bibles to the underground. I learned of a precious Chinese brother who was truly upset that he hadn't yet been jailed and tortured. He felt he "hadn't been counted worthy" since he hadn't suffered for Christ. I looked up that Scripture, which is in Acts 5:40-41:

> *When they had called for the apostles and beaten them, they commanded that they should not speak in the name of Jesus, and let them go. So they departed from the presence of the council, rejoicing that **they were counted worthy to suffer shame for His name.***

Wow! What faith, what joy comes from that total surrender! I have to admit that I'm not sure I'm there yet. Yet I know that, if we can get to that place of total surrender, God can use us in ways we could never imagine. If we can totally surrender to Father God, if we can trust Him and give Him our very lives, then we will be among the most prized and dangerous warriors in God's army. *Adonai, help us to get there!*

WEAPONS THAT ARE NOT CARNAL

We know we're in a battle, and we know the armor God has given us. Now the question is, what do our weapons look like? How does our battle manifest? Second Corinthians 10:4 clarifies this for us when it says, *"For the weapons of our warfare are not carnal but mighty through God to the pulling down of strongholds...."* This is an awesome verse. *Carnal* is translated from the Greek word *sarkikos,* which means "Fleshly...pertaining to the flesh or body, the opposite of pneumatikos." The Greek word *pneumatikos* means "non-carnal...a spirit, or supernatural..."[3] To summarize, our weapons are not physical weapons but are spiritual. Thus, we fight *in the Spirit!*

Paul continues his thought in Second Corinthians, saying,

> *Casting down imaginations and every high thing that exalteth against the knowledge of God, and bringing into captivity every thought to the obedience of Christ* (2 Corinthians 10:5 KJV).

The fact that we need to cast down imaginations shows that it truly is the battlefield of the mind. Thus, we can think of every Scripture verse that becomes real to us (our *rhema* words) as building blocks. As we build up our minds with the Sword of the Lord (the Word), God's truth delivers the final blow to the enemy. Yeshua has already won; He did it for us! We are simply declaring that victory over our lives and situations.

When we understand this, we can confess the truth of Colossians 2:15—*Yeshua, You have spoiled principalities and powers! You made a show of them openly, and You **triumphed** over them! Hallelujah!*

THE WEAPON OF FORGIVENESS

When I was going through my divorce, I experienced one of the biggest trials of my faith, yet it turned out to be an awesome time of growing in my relationship with my heavenly Husband. Through this testing, I was connected to my heavenly Husband like no other time up to that point. God's Holy Spirit became real to me in a whole new way.

During this time, after losing another battle in court, I went to Tennessee, where my mom was living, with my children in tow. I was very upset and as I neared the Clarksville, Tennessee, exit, I heard the words, "Forgive him."

I knew the Holy Spirit was prompting me to forgive my ex-husband. I argued, "No, Lord, I can't. I won't. Can't You see what he's done?"

Again I heard, "Forgive him."

I was getting close to the mall exit, so I pulled off and went into the mall. I pulled out my Gideon Bible and opened it up right there in the mall, in front of God and everybody. I don't remember what verse the Spirit gave me, but I know it was about forgiveness. Right then and there, the Holy Spirit somehow granted me the grace to forgive him. This seemed to set in motion the next set of events. Adonai wasn't finished yet.

The kids and I got back in the car and drove the rest of the way to my mom's house. That evening, I started to feel like I needed to ask forgiveness from my ex-husband's girlfriend! "Oh no, Lord," I said. "I can't do that! They are the ones who did wrong!"

"Yes," He said in my spirit, "you're right, but you have been harboring unforgiveness toward her too." Sometimes it's not fun hearing the Holy Spirit reveal the truth about ourselves to us.

But God wasn't done. "While you're at it," He said, "you need to talk to [your ex-husband] and ask for forgiveness from him too."

I thought, *This is not fair!* But I knew I needed to obey, so I called them and asked them both to forgive me. Did this change anything? As far as I could see, the change was only in my spirit. I truly did not harbor any resentment any longer. Was the fight over? Not by a long shot. But I was obedient, and I truly believe that this prepared me for the next step in my walk with my heavenly Husband.

INTRO: THE HOLY SPIRIT

Just a few days after that, I heard the Lord speaking to me again, saying, "You know Me; you know My Son. Now let Me introduce you to My Holy Spirit." A conference was coming up in an Assemblies of God Church, and I was planning on attending. Looking back, I now see how the Holy Spirit was preparing me for what I would experience there.

Before I share what happened, I need to explain that I am writing with no malice and no shaking of the finger. I'm not here to argue church doctrine. For some people, this story may seem too far out there, but I share my testimony as true and as right as I can remember.

First, some background. I was raised in a Presbyterian church. It was absolutely a good, solid Christian upbringing, and I was born again at the age of 19 due to my pastor's diligence to the Word, some wonderful saints praying for me, and Jesus constantly knocking at my door! I had some good, solid teachings under my belt, but I did not know much about the Holy Spirit, especially related to speaking in tongues.

My children and I ending up temporarily moving to Tennessee on a medical emergency to be with my mom, who had fallen and broken her hip. We started attending a Methodist church. Again, it was a good, solid upbringing in the Word for all of us, but it wasn't a church that practiced speaking in tongues. (This is not true of all denominational churches, whether Presbyterian or Methodist or something else, but it was my experience. Recently I met some awesome Spirit-filled Methodists, and I know there are many others!)

As I was going through the pain of the divorce, *Jehovah-Jireh*—the Lord Who Provides—knew that I needed something more. When He told me He wanted to introduce me to the Holy Spirit, I did not really have any understanding of what that meant. But I knew I needed something more, so I attended the conference at that Assemblies of God church, and it was a wonderful, powerful time of soaking up the Word. I needed it.

Then, in the third session, the pastor talked about the gifts of the Holy Spirit. This was like an introduction for me. When he asked for people to come forward to receive the gifts of the Holy Spirit with the evidence of speaking in tongues, I went forward wanting (even needing) to receive this gift. I could tell that something about that place was different; everything seemed like it was electrically charged.

Some of the conference helpers took the people wanting to receive the Spirit into a room to pray over us. All of a sudden, I started to feel my belly shake. It was unlike anything I had ever experienced before, and it was the most powerful experience with the Holy Spirit that I had ever had up to that point. Yeshua speaks about this (though I did not know this particular Scripture at the time): *"He that believeth on Me, as the scripture hath said, out of his belly shall flow rivers of living water"* (John 7:38 KJV).

What exactly does *living water* mean? It comes from the Greek word *zao,* meaning:

> To live, have physical life and existence...implying always some duration. Generally, of human life. Of persons raised from the dead; of those restored from sickness, not to die. "Living water" means the water of running streams and fountains, as opposed to that of stagnant cisterns, pools or marshes.[4]

Oh, Lord Jesus, give us some of that! We don't need to be stagnant cisterns (yuck!); we want to flow with Your living water!

As the conference helper was speaking to me, she said something like, "Now, just speak it out, just speak it out." Not knowing what this really was, I became too scared to speak. I asked quietly for Father to take it from me because I was overwhelmed. My belly quit shaking, but I still felt like there was an electric charge in the air. That was not the end of the story.

A NEW SEASON

About five years later, my mom had gone home to be with the Lord, my children had moved to their dad's, and a man I had been dating walked away. When all that happened, I felt it was time for a change. My family and I had been attending a Presbyterian church; it was just what we all needed at the time. But once they were gone, I knew I needed to be around more people my age, and I especially needed a church that was practicing the gifts. So, I switched to a nondenominational church that I felt the Holy Spirit was directing me to. It seemed like I had found what I was looking for. *"Ask, and it shall be given you; seek, and ye shall find; knock, the door shall be opened unto you"* (Matt. 7:7 KJV).

One evening, a brother in the Lord was preaching on the gifts and asked those who wanted the gifts of the Holy Spirit with evidence of tongues to come forward. I again went forward because I felt I never received this gift since I never spoke it out a few years earlier in Tennessee. There were several who went up front along with me. As we started to pray and seek the Lord, the brother who was teaching came over and said, "My goodness, this woman is already filled. Just speak it out, speak it out." Well, I did, and I've been speaking it out ever since. Thank You, Father, Son, and Holy Ghost!

The Importance of the Gifts

The gift of tongues is just that—a *gift*. Some teach that people who don't have that gift are not saved. I don't believe the Scriptures teach that. Having Christ in our hearts (see Rom. 10:9) is what gets us to Heaven. Yeshua is our salvation, not the gift of operating in the Spirit.

On the other end of the spectrum are those who believe that the gifts are not in operation today. I don't believe the Scriptures teach that either. Since Yeshua—who is the Word—is the same yesterday, today, and forever (see Heb. 13:8), we can know that the gifts are operating today as they were the day of Pentecost (see Acts 2). Likewise, we can see that the gifts are for both Jewish and Gentile believers. Acts 10:45-46 says:

> *The gift of the Holy Spirit had been poured out on the Gentiles also. For they heard them speak with tongues and magnify God.*

Clearly, the gifts of the Spirit are for all people today just as they were in the early Church.

Many have wondered, "Why are the spiritual gifts so important?" God's holy, inspired Word teaches us to desire spiritual gifts. *"Pursue love and desire spiritual gifts..."* (1 Cor. 14:1). The next verse teaches, *"For he who speaks in a tongue does not speak to men but to God..."* (1 Cor. 14:2). Tongues edify the person who speaks. *Edification* comes from the Greek word *oikodomeo,* which means (figuratively) "to build up, establish, confirm."[5] In these endtimes, we are going to need the power of the Holy Spirit edifying us in order to make it through. This passage also speaks of prophecy, as well as several other gifts of the Spirit. These are highlighted in First Corinthians 12-14.

The most insightful book I've ever read about the working power of the Holy Spirit was written by Dave Roberson: *The Walk of the Spirit— The Walk of Power,* subtitled *The Vital Role of Praying in Tongues.* This was given to me by a friend after I heard Sonja—my powerful sister in the Lord I mentioned in an earlier chapter—teach a message on the Holy Spirit. I highly recommend this book for those who want to read a wonderful testimony and study.

One of the things that stood out when I read it was how satan has deceived many believers into thinking the gifts aren't relevant today. He has done this because he can't fight the Holy Spirit's power; satan is scared of this power. He cannot work while we are operating in the gifts. This is why he has tried to keep believers from working in their gifts, and it is why there is so much division in the Church over it.

THE POWER OF TONGUES

A couple of years ago, I actually had a dream pertaining to this. In the dream, I was walking downtown with a guy friend. We came upon a man and his girlfriend or wife. As we got closer to them, they broke out in a fight right beside us. He pushed her down to the curb and told her how stupid she was. My friend and I both went up to him to get him off of her, but he got up and backed off on his own. My friend was ready to come at him with his fists up, so the man put up his fists. I got in the middle and stopped them and said, "Let's not do this." Then I asked the man if I could pray with him. He answered yes, so we went toward an alley and stood there, not too far from the main sidewalk.

When I started to pray, he kept disrupting. I asked him to stop, but he wouldn't. I looked around to see if anyone was watching; then I got mad at him for disrupting and immediately started praying in tongues. When I did, the power of speaking in tongues backed him up against the wall, and he wasn't able to move or speak. I went to raise my hand to touch him, but felt the Holy Spirit telling me not to touch him. Then a woman (whom I had just worked with that day at a junior high school) came over to talk with me. I wasn't able to talk to her as I was still praying in tongues. She prayed with me and smiled, and we started praising. When I woke up, I was still praying in tongues and shaking.

It was a very powerful dream, and I believe the Holy Spirit Himself was trying to show me how effective this spiritual weapon in our arsenal is. If our prayers in tongues can nail the enemy up against a wall, it is no wonder that satan has worked so hard to get many believers confused and in unbelief about it. The gifts of the Spirit are powerful tools in our battle against the weapons formed against us.

The Weapon of Fasting

Jesus said once, referring to a demon, *"However, this kind does not go out except by prayer and fasting"* (Matt. 17:21). Many people shudder at the word *fasting*. As those who've tried it know, it is not very physically pleasant. However, the rewards are well worth it!

I was not very familiar with fasting until I visited the International House of Prayer (IHOP) in Kansas City. A friend and I visited one of the prophetic teams there, and they strongly recommended that we both start fasting together. One team member said something like, "It is the spark that will start the fire burning." Though I was not too familiar with fasting, my friend was, and we started to fast the next day since that was the day that the ministry teams at IHOP were fasting. It was a great motivation.

I recently called Rabbi Laurie and asked about fasting. He explained, "Christians have gotten into all these different kinds of fasts; however, the Jewish people had specific fasts at specific times." I'm not going to go into all of the Jewish fasts here. The main point Rabbi wanted to get across was that fasts are to *"separate yourself from the flesh"* and to *"get out of your own way!"* One type of Jewish fast goes from sundown to the next sundown. I have tried to do this fast one day a week since my visit to IHOP.

I've seen Christians do all types of fasts. Some will fast for a day, three days, a week, ten days (see Dan. 1), or even 40 days (see Matt. 4:2). Many cannot do a complete fast from food due to health issues. Some may fast television or movies. The key is doing whatever we feel led to do by the Holy Spirit. However, it also helps to plan ahead and do it with a friend or two. Having a purpose in mind related to what we need to separate from (our sinful flesh) is also helpful. The more like-focused our fasting partners are, the more successful we will be.

Like-minded individuals will help keep us on track! I once went on a 40-day vegetarian fast with a couple of friends (of course, this only works for those who eat meat). It was a very focused and cleansing time for all. The ultimate goal was to kill the flesh and wholly focus on the Holy One of Israel. Fasting is another very powerful tool in our arsenal as we zero in during our battles.

A LESSON FROM JEHOSHAPHAT

We might all learn a lesson in how to handle adversity from Jehoshaphat. When he became the king of Judah, he did some major clean-up work in the land. He removed idols and images and prepared himself and his subjects to seek God. He set new reforms, new courts and judges, in motion, telling them to *"...act in the fear of the Lord, faithfully and with a loyal heart"* (2 Chron. 19:9).

As he was seeking and doing God's will, a battle started to brew. Enemies from surrounding lands were poised with their armies to wipe out the king and his people. I can just hear his people in a panic screaming, "The Moabites are coming! The Ammonites are coming! What shall we do?" The king could have cried out, "Oh Lord, what have You done to us? Why have You allowed this? I have cleaned up Your land. I have followed Your ways. Why are You doing this?" The Word says he was scared! I would have been too. But instead of running around in a panic:

> *Jehoshaphat...set himself to seek the Lord, and proclaimed a fast throughout all Judah. So, Judah gathered together to ask help from the Lord; and from all the cities of Judah they came to seek the Lord* (2 Chronicles 20:3-4).

After the king and the people assembled and stated their case to their Maker, they prayed this amazing prayer of faith,

> *O our God, will You not judge them? For we have no power against this great multitude that is coming against us; nor do we know what to do, but our eyes are upon You* (2 Chronicles 20:12).

What great faith! *Our eyes are upon You, Father God. We look to You. You are our Strength, our Defender, our Shield in this battle.* This should always be our prayer in the battle! Look what happens next. The Spirit of the Lord came swooping in and spoke through a prophet:

> *Do not be afraid nor dismayed because of this great multitude, for the battle is not yours, but God's....Position yourselves, stand still and see the salvation of the Lord, who is with you...Do not fear or be dismayed...the Lord is with you* (2 Chronicles 20:15,17).

God has a plan to save us in our battles too. Just look at all the tools that Adonai has given us to win the war: praise, prayer, the armor, faith, forgiveness, belief, righteousness, the gifts of the Holy Spirit, angels, and even fasting. The main thing is to always seek the Lord God first, to desire Him first. He is the Giver of the gifts, the Lover of our souls. Our Husband, our Companion, our Partner knows what we need, and He desires to lavish upon us His gifts. *He* longs to do it. As we fight spiritual battles, as we walk through this life, He longs to bless us! Yeshua, while talking about people giving good gifts to their children, said, *"How much more will your Father who is in Heaven give good things to those who ask Him?"* (Matt. 7:11). Luke quotes Jesus's words also, but adds, *"How much more shall your heavenly Father give the Holy Spirit to them that ask Him?"* (Luke 11:13 KJV).

Those who are still seeking the gifts of the Spirit must simply ask. Yeshua, who is the Author and Finisher of our faith (see Heb. 12:2), will do it! *Thank You, King Yeshua!*

Prayer Nugget

Precious Lord, You are such a great and awesome God. There is none like You, Father. We give You praise in the battle. You are our Warrior Husband who comes forth like a Mighty Man! Establish our hearts, Father, when "they" assemble so that we shall be able to withstand. For You are fighting for us! Establish our children and our loved ones, Adonai. Establish us, Holy Father, in faith, forgiveness, belief, righteousness, and the gifts of Your Holy Spirit.

When we become weary, beat-up, or discouraged, Your strength is made perfect in our weakness. Help us to put on Your armor; help us to stand. Lord Jesus, this is why You were made manifest, to destroy the works of the devil. Hallelujah!

Adonai—our Lord and Master—we ask for wisdom, for insight in this battle. We need mountain-moving faith! Go before us, and be our Rear-Guard, our Defender, our Shield, and our Buckler.

We claim that no weapon formed against us or our loved ones shall prosper.

Count us worthy as we suffer for Your sake. Thank You for the awesome power of the Holy Spirit. You are the Author and Finisher of our faith! Perfect us, Father God. For those seeking the gifts, Your gifts, Father, we ask, and it shall be given, we seek and find, we knock and the door will be opened. Through it all, Abba Father, help us to love others, to forgive others, and to walk in obedience and discernment through Your Holy Spirit. Thank You, Yeshua! Amen!

ENDNOTES

1. *The Hebrew-Greek Key Word Study Bible KJV* (Chattanooga, TN: AMG Publishers, 2008), commentary on "alethia" in Ephesians 6:14.

2. Ibid., commentary on "righteousness" in Ephesians 6:14.

3. Nelson NKJV Study Bible (Nashville, TN: Thomas Nelson), commentary on "sarkikos"; "pneumatikos" in 2 Corinthians 10:4.

4. *The Hebrew-Greek Key Word Study Bible KJV,* commentary on "zao" in John 7:38.

5. Ibid., commentary on "oikodomeo" in 1 Corinthians 14:2.

PERSONAL
Notes

Chapter Eight

NEW BEGINNINGS

This is the heritage of the servants of the Lord... (Isaiah 54:17).

Victory is here! Victory is from the Lord; it is our heritage! He's already given us the victory—now let's walk in it.

Just like the Israelites, we have come through the battle. This is Chapter 8, and the number eight symbolizes "new beginnings." We have come out of bondage and are now looking toward future redemption. Even Hashem says:

> *For behold, I am bringing forth a new miracle! Now it will sprout, you will surely know it: I will make a road in the desert and in the wilderness rivers* (Isaiah 43:19 Tanach).

Just a few chapters ago, we were talking about the wilderness. Yet thankfully, the wilderness does not last forever. Victory is the heritage of God's children. Something new is now happening. For those of us who are in need of a miracle right now, our Husband is telling us that one is about to spring up. Our way is about to be opened. I like how the NIV states Isaiah 43:19, *"See, I am doing a new thing...do you not perceive it?"*

Yeshua went through a test in the wilderness, not unlike many of us, but He came out victorious, and we too can come through in victory. He will bring forth a new thing—a new miracle! This is a promise from our Husband. I wonder what new plan He has in store for those who have continued looking to Him, even in the wilderness?

UNREALISTIC OPTIMISM?

Years ago I had a close friend and prayer partner who found herself with many huge struggles. As I listened to her, I began musing over several statements she made. I was not trying to point a finger but just trying to search out the heart of the matter and help her because she was asking for help. It was easy on the outside, to see what was going on in her and her family's lives, but when we are the ones in the battle, it can be difficult to see the forest for the trees.

I told this friend at one point (we were emailing back and forth) that I was thinking about and then chuckling over her statement, "I'm tired of being sickly optimistic." I answered with, "What is the alternative here? To be sickly depressed? Let's see—crying all the time, feeling sorry for ourselves, antidepressants. Hmmmmm...I'll stick with sickly optimistic, thank you very much."

I went on to explain, "So, what does that mean? I too realize that it seems like we Christians are toooooo optimistic. So I'm thinking this is crazy—to be all the time hoping, optimistic, not even being real about what *is* going on. Then I thought, *Well, I'll just become a realist then. I'm being too optimistic.* But then as I realized what *is* going on in my life, and at just the realization of that—wow!—I was becoming depressed! So, I had to rise above, and say, 'I choose to search for hope, choose to search the deep things of God, choose to abide under the shadow of His wings. I even choose to let *Him* love me, to receive His love for me. And in that deep *love,* if there is discipline *He* has to do and things *He* has to weed out of my life, I choose *life!*"

I truly believe that is how I was healed. I died to self; I didn't put my hope anywhere else. And in that place, Yeshua met me and restored hope.

WHY THIS SUFFERING?

My friend had also voiced her concern about "all the suffering, suffering, suffering." I answered her, "Yeshua Himself says, *'You will always have the poor among you...'* (Matt. 26:11). Did you know that Yeshua feels? I have always disagreed with the statement, 'It's not about how you feel.' Well, sometimes it is. If Yeshua hadn't had enough feeling to have compassion on us, where would we be? The Word says, *'He* [Yeshua] *was moved with compassion for them, and healed their sick'* (Matt. 14:14)."

That compassion should move us into action. Compassion begins to put the healing process in motion. When Yeshua walked this earth, He had compassion, and that compassion moved Him to act. When He acted out His compassion, it became love in action. *Love* is a verb; He acted that out, and we must *know* that He still gives out that healing love today! The fact that He died on the cross, rose again, and healed us from our dying, hopeless condition is enough! The Greek word for *save* is *sozo; actually *sozo* means "saved, healed and delivered."[1] This gives a whole new meaning to the billboard phrase that says "Jesus Saves," doesn't it?

We must talk to God to see where we need to feel that heartbeat that He has for His children. At times our emotions can start overtaking us and make us ineffective to ourselves and to others. This is when the statement, "It's not about how you feel," starts coming into play. At those times, we need to seek Him and seek to understand what His Word says about us when the destroyer is trying to destroy us. So in a sense it's true that we can't rely on feelings but on what He has already made known to us.

Let's speak it out, brave hearts. Let's get out our Swords and speak. "I am the head and not the tail, above only and not beneath (see Deut. 28:13). I am more than a conqueror through Him that loved us (see Rom. 8:37). I am an overcomer (see Rev. 2:7). I can do all things through Christ who strengthens me (see Phil. 4:13)!"

If you're wallowing a little too long in the stressed, overwhelmed, anxious, and depressed department, you may have to simply believe and trust in your Husband and His Word and simply choose to change your countenance by faith. I know I've had to change mine more than a few times.

Why are you cast down, O my soul? And why are you disquieted within me? Hope in God; for I shall yet praise Him, the help of my countenance and my God (Psalm 42:11).

C. S. Lewis (I'm a huge fan of his) has a good word about our sufferings, anxieties, and afflictions. He eloquently says,

> Some people feel guilty about their anxieties and regard them as a defect of faith, but they are afflictions, not sins. Like all afflictions, they are, if we can so take them, our share in the passion of Christ.[2]

UNANSWERED PRAYERS?

Finally, my friend wondered, "Why doesn't the Lord answer prayers?" Of course, I *know* that He does. I answered with, "I'm still here, pain free, so I'm living proof." I told her that I was going to "pull out a maryism on this—'You can't heal till you get real.'" God knows everything, and He honors obedience more than sacrifice. Yeshua wants to heal our finances, emotions, self-esteem issues, family obstacles, and health—wants to heal every area of our life! It says in Matthew 8 that a leper walked up to Yeshua and worshiped Him, saying, *"Lord, if You are willing, You can make me clean."* Yeshua said, *"I am willing, be cleansed"* (Matt. 8:2-3). He *is* willing; we have to believe that! Thank You, Yeshua!

I ended the email to my friend with these words: "Prayin' for ya, pullin' for ya, pressin' in for ya, standin' in the gap for ya, lovin' ya." I suggested she check out the Book of Ecclesiastes, and I told her, "I believe we go through seasons, and this is a season you're going through. That's all."

She had become tired of waiting, of hoping. When our hopes are dashed and disappointments arise, our insecurities seem to flourish. But if we don't have hope anymore, what do we have? Hopelessness. *"Hope deferred makes the heart sick..."* (Prov. 13:12). Unfortunately, at that time in her life, my friend chose to quit hoping. She has since moved to another state, and we have lost touch, but my prayers go with her and her family that someday she will return to the hope found in Yeshua.

I spoke recently with another friend who told me she doesn't hear from God right now—she is feeling empty. That is a season too. That's when we learn to just be still and know that He is God (see Ps. 46:10). In our stillness, in our quiet place, is where we begin to hear, to know. I continued to remind this friend that "we know the Word, it's in our hearts and our minds, so when the feeling is not there, that's when we should just be still and know that He is." I believe such times are testing times in which we need to draw up His Word and put His faithfulness in our remembrance (see Isa. 43:26).

Box Full of Prayers

A few years ago I had an experience that continues to speak to me about the power of prayer. I had been waking up in mild panic attacks at 3:00 A.M. on consecutive nights. After the third night, it seemed the attack was increasing in intensity, and I cried out, "Help me, Jesus." I finally went back to sleep and had this dream: I was in a room full of people I didn't know. We had gathered to pray, and prayer requests were being taken. As one man started to share, he broke down and started crying. A few of us (men and women) went over to try and comfort him. I was directly behind him, and I put my hands on his shoulders (he was sitting down). As we were praying, he seemed to relax and started to let the Holy Spirit minister to him.

At that point, my feet suddenly came up off the ground, and it scared me. I was wondering if I was levitating and if it was of God. I realized that two angels were on each side, gently lifting me but waiting on *my* decision to let go. I grabbed onto the man's shoulders harder. I was trying to decide if this was God or satan. Then I thought, *Wait a minute. I'm in the Spirit here*, and I felt like I needed to trust and let go and let God.

When I did, I immediately was whisked up and away at an extremely fast speed. The others in the prayer room were watching the whole thing unfold. The roof in the room had opened up as I was being lifted. I could actually feel the movement as we headed up through a starry sky. A couple of times there was actually turbulence as we hit a couple of rough spots, but all in all, I thought it was a pretty fun ride! I was excitedly thinking, *It's happening! It's really happening! I'm being taken up to Heaven!*

The angels gently landed me down on a platform of some type. I was facing an old (like back in the ancient Hebrew days) building. It had an open doorway framed by old, thick wood, and there was a man kneeling and praying over a gold box that was open. The gold box seemed to be actual gold with some scrolling or etching on the sides. It was square and big enough to hold a couple pairs of large boots. The top was open, and in it were pieces of paper. I perceived them to be my prayer requests. The box seemed to be lined with red velvet or even silk. The man was dressed in ancient Hebrew garb, clothed in linen with a turban on his head. (Later, I soon found out that in Exodus 28:37 it talks about turbans that Aaron and his sons were told to wear.)

I felt like he was a godly man and was praying over my prayer requests. He was praying in another language, and I asked for interpretation, but realized that even if I could understand him, I wouldn't be able to hear him well enough. I started to wake up, yet I was feeling angry, as I didn't want to leave this place. Upon waking, though, the peace of God covered me, and I realized that if I didn't quit being angry, the peace was going to leave. So I let the peace wash over me and went back to sleep.

The next morning, I called my "dream interpreter," Brother David. After I shared my dream with him, he said he had the interpretation. The priest was the ancient order of Melchizedek (see Gen. 14; Heb. 5). These priests are said to "re-pray" our prayers to Father. Brother David said that the Lord was trying to encourage me by showing me that my prayers are being heard. The message of the dream is to keep praying, to keep being faithful, and to keep believing that my petitions before the Lord are not forgotten. Thank You, Adonai! I still contemplate that dream from time to time, and I have always felt that, as the box gets completely full of prayer requests and starts to run over, that I receive the promise from Yeshua:

"Give, and it will be given unto you: good measure, pressed down, shaken together, and running over..." (Luke 6:38).

Hang in there. Your prayers are being heard. I believe (as I was shown) that they are being prayed over again in Heaven as you are being faithful to believe, keep praying, and serve others. Wow! The privilege of prayer is absolutely essential in the lives of servants of the Lord—it is the heritage of those who seek Him!

GOD-RIGHTEOUSNESS OR SELF-RIGHTEOUSNESS

"And their righteousness is from Me," says the Lord (Isaiah 54:17).

Righteousness is a difficult subject to talk about. Sometimes I feel like I'm the least-righteous person I know. I want to spit myself out, knowing my righteousness is like filthy rags (see Isa. 64:6). I know I am covered by the blood of Yeshua and that He makes me righteous, yet in the midst of life, it can all seem like yada yada yada to me. I'm sure many believers can relate to this struggle with the word *righteousness*. We know the Word is true but our problem is just that we often don't fully understand what it means for us in our day-to-day lives.

Let's examine *righteousness* in the light of what many confuse it with—their own *self-righteousness*. A few weeks ago, I turned on the radio to a Christian program about addictions. The man talking said that in the United States, one in three people will have an addiction of some kind. He even included "addicted to self" in his list of example addictions. What this means is that, even if we personally are not dealing with addiction, we are dealing with someone in our family or circle of friends who is.

Within a day or two of when I heard that radio program, a prophetic friend of mine called to say that she had gone to hear an evangelist speak. She said he spoke of having a dream and felt Father was clearly speaking to him about what was hurting His heart most. It was not so much the sin issues Christians all face, but that so many Christians are shaking their fingers at those who are struggling. The Church has lost its compassion, and this man felt it is breaking Father's heart. Too many are lost in their own self-righteousness and are busy hurting the souls who need compassion. Christians getting wounded in the battle by "friendly fire" is not our Maker's plan.

Dear hearts, whether you've been wounded outside the Church walls or inside of them, do whatever it takes to get yourself healthy. Get back in Church even though you have been hurt by "church people." Quit looking to them and start looking to Him—your Maker, your Husband. There are also wonderful Christian-based counseling and inner healing programs out there. Refusing to deal with these hurts will only hurt you and keep you from your potential.

For many years, I suppressed a lot of my hurt from years past, and at one point I so isolated myself because of all the hurt and the pain I was in that I began to wonder if I was going to be able to pull myself out. I too had begun to lose hope. My hope had been deferred one too many times, it seemed. But my Husband, my God, sent someone who recognized that I was in "great grief" (his words) and encouraged me to get into a program called Celebrate Recovery.

Celebrate Recovery provides a way to deal with our "hurts, habits, and hang-ups." I knew this was for me. Through the program, I gained new friends, and I was being pulled out of the wilderness. For some reason, I thought I just might stay there. But the Man with the plan had a different thought. John 16:33 records Yeshua's words:

> *These things I have spoken to you, that in Me you may have peace. In the world you will have tribulation; but be of good cheer, I have overcome the world.*

Our righteousness is from Yeshua, and He even gives us peace. Our Husband even overcame the world for us; it sounds like a victory plan to me!

GRACE FOR RIGHTEOUSNESS

Righteousness is a gift from our Husband! My eyes opened up when I caught this verse in Romans 5:17:

> *For if by the one man's offense death reigned through the one, much more those who receive abundance of grace and of the gift of righteousness will reign in life through the One, Jesus Christ.*

Death (sin) came through the one man—Adam. But we have received an *"abundance of grace"* (there's that wonderful word *grace* again) and the *"gift of righteousness"* through the One—the only One—*Christ Himself.*

"Scripture set in motion," is what I keep hearing as we're finishing up the last chapter. God wants to set His Scripture in motion—that lovely, breathing Word flowing through our lives. It guides us and protects us. This has been a journey of living, breathing testimonies set on paper. I hope it inspires you to reach out to no one or no thing but our Maker, our Husband. Through His Word, He has given us grace as His righteousness flows through us. What a wonderful gift!

GREAT COMPASSION

If I learned anything about our heavenly Father and Husband while compiling this book, it is the depth of *His compassion for us.* He is truly near to the broken-hearted. He is near to us in our mess-ups. I have experienced His (and only His) depth of compassion, His deep and unending love. When others have refused to acknowledge my hurts or have tried to tell me I wasn't trusting Him, when people I loved abandoned ship and flippantly said, "It's God's will," I was amazed at how Abba Father would take the time to minister to my hurts in a way no one else could.

He weeps with us, and He acknowledges our honest cry. He sent me friends with shoulders to cry on. He even took the time to send me dreams to show me that He was acknowledging my hurt—He understood. The validation I received from Him, speaking as my Lover, Husband, and

Healer was enough to get me through. It was as if He was saying, "I see you, My child. I see you, My love. I see your hurt and pain, and I am with you." And I say, "Thank You, Father. Thank You, Lord Yeshua."

He is with us through the dark, cold winters of our lives. We may not even realize He's there because we are hurting so, but He is, and He is saying, *"Rise up, my love, my fair one, and come away. For, lo, the winter is past, the rain is over and gone; the flowers appear...the time of the singing of birds is come..."* (Song of Sol. 2:10-12 KJV). The Bride (representative of the Church) replies in verse 16, *"My beloved is mine and I am His..."* Let that be our heart song to the Lover of our souls. Hear Him saying, "Rise up My beloved; rise up My love. The winter is over. Spring is here. Can't you hear the lovely song of the birds? Rise up! Rise up!"

A SONG OF LOVE

I started having dreams about apples recently. In the second dream, I had to clean up *cinnamon apples* lying all over the place. I was not happy. The morning after the second dream, the Tanach fell off its stand and onto my foot. Why it didn't hurt, I'll never know, but what I do know is that Father was trying to tell me something—*read!* I decided to look up all the Scriptures I could find on *apples*. God put me in the Song of Solomon again. I had never had that Book opened up to me (speaking to me) in such a way before. The whole Book was becoming a *rhema* word as I began learning in a whole new way to seek God as my Husband and the Lover of my soul.

I pray this opens up for all of us, that we all get a glimpse of the Song because that is where we enter the secret chamber, the throne room of God. In that place, we know that nothing else matters, but His love for us. As I mentioned previously, Song of Solomon is an allegory for how Christ loves His Church. *We* are the Church. Let's allow His Word to sing over us in the following quote from the Stone Edition Tanach:

> *Like the fruitful, fragrant apple among the barren trees of the forest, so is my Beloved among the gods. In His shade I delighted*

and there I sat, and the fruit of His Torah [the first five books of the Bible] *was sweet to my palate. He brought me to the chamber of Torah and delights and clustered my encampments about Him in love. I say to Him, "Sustain me in exile with dainty cakes, spread fragrant apples about me to comfort my dispersion, for bereft of Your Presence, I am sick with love." With memories of His loving support in the desert* [this spoke to me of my wilderness place], *of His left hand under my head, of His right hand enveloping me* (Song of Solomon 2:3-6).

Wow, Lord Jesus! Wow! I have to keep going:

If you violate your oath, you will become as defenseless as gazelles in a field...if you dare to provoke God to hate me or disturb His love for me while He still desires it. The voice of my Beloved! Behold, it came suddenly to redeem me, as if leaping over mountains, skipping over hills. In His swiftness to redeem me, my Beloved is like a gazelle...I thought I would be forever alone, but behold! He was standing behind our wall, observing through the windows, peering through the lattices (Song of Solomon 2:7-9).

Can't you just see our precious Love wooing us? This passage is like two star-crossed lovers playing hide and seek! Let's read on:

At the sea, He said to me "O My dove, trapped at the sea as if in the clefts of the rock, the concealment of the terrace. Show Me your prayerful gaze, [But Lord, I can't see for tears!] *let Me hear your supplicating voice* [But Lord, I can't speak] *for your voice is sweet and your countenance comely." My Beloved is mine, He fills all my needs and I seek from Him and none other. He grazes me in roselike bounty. Until my sin blows His friendship away... My sin causes Him to turn away* (Song of Solomon 2:14-17).

This is powerful stuff! Let's look now at the beginning of the next chapter, after Hashem has been aloof because of our sins:

I grasped Him, determined that my deeds would never again cause me to lose hold of Him, until I brought His Presence to the Tabernacle of my mother and to the chamber of the one who conceived me (Song of Solomon 3:4).

I will go to Mount Moriah and the hill of frankincense—where you will be completely fair, My beloved, and no blemish will be in you. You have captured My heart, My sister, O bride, you have captured My heart with but one of your virtues... (Song of Solomon 4:6-7).

This is amazing! He's talking to us! He's saying that *we* have captured His heart!

As chaste as a garden locked, My sister, O bride, a spring locked up, a fountain sealed. Your least gifted ones are a pomegranate orchard with luscious fruit...calamus and cinnamon... (Song of Solomon 4:12-13).

I'm no longer angry that I had to clean up cinnamon apples in my dream.

Despite my laments in exile, His left hand supports my head and His right hand embraces me...How worthy she is descending from the wilderness bearing Torah and His Presence, clinging to her Beloved... (Song of Solomon 8:3,5).

Yes, Lord, we cling to Your Word and to Your presence!

Flee, My Beloved, from our common exile and be like a gazelle or a young hart in Your swiftness to redeem and rest Your Presence among us on the fragrant Mount Moriah, site of Your Temple (Song of Solomon 8:14).

I am in *awe* of these passages! When I read these, I had just come from worshipping at a place in Poplar Bluff, Missouri, called Moriah Ranch.

Had I been reading from any other version than the Tanach, I would have missed the Moriah reference!

"It Is Sufficient"

God is no respecter of persons (see Acts 10:34). He shows no partiality, and He is with us in our many afflictions and trials. At one time, I had the feeling that the good gifts of God (healing, promotion, joy, and so forth) were for other people and that He didn't have anything for me. This is a lie. May we all be free from such thoughts, free to believe that He honors and remembers our honest cry to Him. He tells us, *"Put Me in remembrance: let us plead together: declare though, that thou mayest be justified"* (Isa. 43:26 KJV). The Tanach starts this verse with *"Remind Me..."*

We must quit thinking, when we hear of someone else's breakthrough, *Oh that's only for them; God has nothing for me.* That's a lie from the devil himself. Our blessed Lord and Savior honors our realness before Him; we can bring our complaints to the Lord. The Bible promises, *"Evening, morning and at noon will I utter my complaint and moan and sigh, and **He will hear my voice"*** (Ps. 55:17). This, of course, is not to be confused with complaining to others *about* God and not having faith in the bondage breaker. Such an attitude kept the Israelites wandering in the desert for 40 years. Complaining because we lack faith does not please God; sharing our hearts with Him, including the pain and the questions, does.

Recently, I attended a Seder, the Jewish observance of the Passover remembering the exodus from Egypt. This was celebrated by Christ at the time of His Last Supper. Yeshua was and is the Passover Lamb! We learned a song called "Dayenu." Rabbi Laurie taught that if the Israelites would have learned early on to quit complaining (to each other about God) they wouldn't have had all the problems they encountered. He encouraged us, in *whatever* circumstance we are in, to say "Dayenu—it is sufficient." Lord Father, teach us to say "Dayenu!"

A REMNANT

The Book of Isaiah closely mirrors our own Christian life. Obedience, disobedience, a falling away, then a turning back (repent!) to God, and redemption comes again. It's a cycle that unfortunately repeats itself—but it is a trial, and if we learn our lessons well, we won't have to keep wandering around in the hot, dry, and thirsty desert.

In chapters 1 through 39, Isaiah "delivered his message of condemnation to the eighth-century Israelites, pronouncing judgment on their immoral and idolatrous lifestyles."[3] It seems like our current culture has crossed that line too.

In chapters 40 through 55 (Isaiah 54 falls in this group), we see Isaiah comforting "the future generation of weary exiles."[4] No wonder I have always felt such comfort in Isaiah 54. Starting with the first verse, our own Abba Father is telling us to sing, to praise Him. Yet He is talking to the widows, the orphans, the divorced, the down-trodden, the left behind, the forsaken, the forgotten—the very ones who might not feel like praising Him. He is talking to us!

Isaiah finishes with a third section, chapters 56 through 66. Most scholars believe the temple was being rebuilt during the period of this last group of chapters (see Isa. 66:1), and the Israelites were looking forward to the promised Messiah and the time when the "Gentiles would join Israel's godly remnant to become the 'servants' of the Lord."[5] Rebuild *our* temples in this last hour, Lord Jesus; ready those who are left, and steady Your bride as we await Your return!

Israel is the remnant that is left! We are that remnant that is left! Our children are that remnant that is left! God always leaves a remnant—that is a promise and a hope and a future for us all. *"Even so then, at this present time there is a remnant according to the election of grace"* (Rom. 11:5). Here is that beautiful, wonderful word *grace* again. This chapter in Romans warns us:

Do not boast against the branches [Israel]. *But if you do boast, remember that you do not support the root, but the root supports you* (Romans 11:18).

This is why replacement theology (which teaches that the Church replaces the Jewish people) doesn't work. The Israelites are still under God's covenant to Abraham—God's covenant with them. We, as the Church, are grafted in along with them. Praise Him for that!

CRACKED POTS

I recently visited a dear brother in the Lord—one of my spiritual mentors—who was recently transferred to the Veteran's Administration hospital. He came within an inch of his life when he fell out a second-story window onto a bed of concrete. Just about everything was shattered but his spirit. He knows that he is only alive by God's grace and mercy.

As we were catching up, I told him about this book based on Isaiah 54—*"Thy Maker is thine Husband."* Knowing the contents of Isaiah 54, Brother Charles lovingly reminded me that Yeshua is the only perfect vessel who has ever walked this earth. One of his favorite things to say is, "God uses cracked pots." Then he reminded me that God now uses imperfect, broken vessels to carry on His work. He knows a lot of my story already; he knows that I am a cracked pot. I looked incredulously at Brother Charles when he said, "God only uses broken vessels," because he was the epitome of a broken vessel—with pretty much everything broken or bruised but his left arm! But the Master Potter is our Great Physician, as well; He knows how to mend us back together.

Why does the Maker of the universe use imperfect and broken vessels (us) to deliver a holy and perfect Word? I think it relates back to that word *relationship*. When we are broken—whether spiritually, physically, or mentally—Father knows that's when we'll seek Him, especially when all else fails!

Sometimes we wonder why we go through these tests. Recently I saw a commercial about adopting abused and left-behind dogs from the pound. It said something like, "Don't feel sorry for them. They are the lucky ones. They are the wise ones—the ones with tales to tell, stories to write." When I first heard it, I thought, *That's it! I'm a pound puppy! I have tales to tell; I have stories to write!* When we come through our battles, we are wiser and stronger, and we have lessons and testimonies to share with others. It is *our* testimony (see Rev. 12:11), and it is how we overcome! *The battle scars can become badges of honor for those who heal and move on to help those who hurt.* We may be like Esther—created for such a time as this! (See Esther 4:14.)

The great faith chapter, Hebrews 11, speaks of those who suffer *"that they might obtain a better resurrection"* (Heb. 11:35). Look at Moses, Sarah, David, and the others in the great cloud of witnesses. Those who have gone before us stood strong in the face of the battle. Brave hearts, through their testimony, we can know that our suffering is for something better.

> *We are surrounded by so great a cloud of witnesses, let us lay aside every weight, and the sin which so easily ensnares us, and let us run with endurance the race that is set before us, looking unto Jesus, the author and finisher of our faith, who for the joy that was set before Him, endured the cross, despising the shame, and has sat down at the right hand of God the Father* (Hebrews 12:1-2).

Victory is our heritage; we will overcome through the power and grace of our Husband Maker.

PRAYER NUGGET

Awesome God our Father, we have been created for such a time as this. Father, let us rest in knowing that our suffering is for a better resurrection. Use us, Lord God, to help others in their times of testing. Bring forth a new thing, a new miracle in our lives as You make a way in the wilderness. Father, we ask You to rain down righteousness, faith, hope, and love into our lives. Help us to step into our royal position; we are called as Your holy priesthood. Through the shed blood of Yeshua, this is ours. Let us not back down, but be bold.

We come to You with truly repentant and broken hearts, Father. Please restore to us the years the locust and the cankerworm have eaten. Sing over us with Your love, precious One. May we enter Your great throne room, the secret chamber, for it's there that You, our Lord, our Husband, will restore our joy and our peace. Thank You for the heritage and righteousness that is ours through the restorative power and blood of Your precious Son, Yeshua. It's in Your precious name we pray, amen.

ENDNOTES

1. James Strong, *Strong's Exhaustive Concordance* (Peabody, MA: Henrickson Publishers), Greek #4982.

2. C.S. Lewis, "C.S. Lewis Quotes"; http://famouspoetsand-poems.com/poets/c__s__lewis/quotes; accessed August 10, 2011.

3. Nelson NKJV Study Bible (Nashville, TN: Thomas Nelson), commentary on the Book of Isaiah.

4. Ibid.

5. Ibid.

PERSONAL
Notes

CONCLUSION

As we close, I hope this book study has left you with new insight and hope. Joel (like Isaiah) was another prophet whom Father God used to speak to His people. The prophet Joel proclaimed a warning to repent, fast, weep, and turn back to God! If we have that truly repentant heart, then Adonai will restore our hope:

> *And I will restore to you the years that the locust have eaten, the cankerworm...Ye shall eat in plenty, and be satisfied, and praise...* (Joel 2: 25-26 KJV).

Look at what's in store for us who believe! This is our heritage. Look at our bloodline! We belong to Father Abraham, to our mother, Sarah. We also belong to Yeshua, who gave it all for us! We believe in Him and gain righteousness—from our Husband Himself. Thank You, Lord Jesus! Thank You!

He is doing a new thing now as you come to Him with a truly repentant and redeemed heart. Claim it for yourself, dear one. *"And He that sat upon the throne said, 'Behold, I make all things new...Write: for these words are true and faithful'"* (Revelation 21:5).

> *"...This is the heritage of the servants of the Lord, and their righteousness is from Me," says the Lord* (Isaiah 54:17).

Amen!

SALVATION MESSAGE

The greatest joy of all is to know Yeshua as your Lord and Savior. First, know that He loves *you!* John 3:16 says:

> *For God so loved the world, that He gave His only begotten Son, that whosoever believeth in Him should not perish, but have everlasting life* (KJV).

See the words *"should not perish"*? You have a choice to make. Those who believe in Him will not perish. Romans 10:11 puts it this way: *"Whoever believeth on Him shall not be ashamed"* (KJV).

Choosing to sin and disobey God separates you from Him. As Romans 3:23 says, *"For all have sinned and fall short of the glory of God."* God knew that all people would need a Savior; that's why He sent His Son. *"Jesus said to him, 'I am the way, the truth, and the life. No one comes to the Father except through Me'"* (John 14:6).

So how do you come to know Him? Romans 10:9-10 says:

> *If you confess with your mouth the Lord Jesus and believe in your heart that God has raised Him from the dead, you will be saved. For with the heart one believes unto righteousness, and with the mouth confession is made unto salvation.*

SALVATION PRAYER:

Father God, I know I am a sinner, and I ask You to forgive me for all my sins. I believe Christ died for me and has forgiven me. Jesus, please come into my heart right now and cleanse me from all unrighteousness. I want You to be my personal Lord and Savior. In the precious name of Jesus I pray, amen!

He loves you, loves you, loves you, and *no one* can ever take that away! Hallelujah!

I strongly encourage and pray for you to find a church to get connected with to help you in your new walk with the Lord.

MY HUSBAND

Submitted will, loving embrace,
My Love, my Husband take me up to Your chamber.
You have swept me off my feet, and I am forever enchanted by
Your endless Grace—Your endless Mercy.
My Beloved is mine and I am His.
My embittered soul was ready to take me down to despair...
But what? My Love, my Husband has come to rescue me.
You extend Your hand of forgiveness and patiently wait for me to look up.
As I do, I gaze upon Your strength, Your beauty, my Love.
As I reach out, Your strong but gentle grip lifts me to You,
So I stand on solid ground—Your embrace envelops me,
surrounds me, Loves me.
Your sweet breath upon me brings life to my being, my soul.
It sets me ablaze. You steady me with Your gaze—You wipe
away my tears. I see Your lips form, and I hear You whisper, "I Love
you." I cannot even fathom the depth of Your Love for me, and as my eyes
tear, I whisper back, "I Love You."
Submitted will, loving embrace.

—POEM BY MARY ELLIOTT

PRECIOUS VESSEL

Oh my precious clay—the vessel of my heart,

I see you lying in sorrow hurting from your fall,

I have loved you, and I have held you next to my heart and face,

And when My creation is grieving, I also share the pain.

The hands that held your affection did not hold you in My sweet grace,

Nor did they consider your well-being as they abandoned you in your state.

Their vision for you was earthly as they limited you in ways,

By judging this Potter's vessel like a prisoner bound in chains,

But I am the God of creation—I see no hopeless state,

Just the working hands of My forgiveness,

Redeeming the Potter's clay.

—POEM BY DEBORAH ESTES
Illustrator

PASSION FOR PURITY PLAN

1. Refuse Unequal Yoking

As a Christian, you are not to be "unequally yoked" (see 2 Cor. 6:14). Many believers think they can "win them over," but what usually happens is that the unbeliever "wins" as the Christian walks away from Christ.

2. Be Friends First

You are brothers and sisters in the Lord. Treat each other as such! You will get to know one another better without the emotional and physical involvement.

3. Set Physical Boundaries

If you find, after dating as friends, that you are both marriage material and that the relationship is becoming serious, set boundaries for your physical relationship. For most (probably all) people, kissing leads to other things. If you *are* pushing that line, but not going "all the way," you have to ask yourself whether you are really giving your best to God. Don't buy into the lie, "We might as well do it since we're going to get married anyway."

Sticking to only hand-holding and hugging seems to be the ticket to not getting caught up in somewhere you don't want to be. Jesus said, *"If you love Me, keep My commandments"* (John 14:15). Kind of hits you where it hurts, doesn't it?

Are you *passionately in love* with *your Savior* enough to *obey* the commandment *"You shall not commit adultery"* (Deut. 5:18)? Yeshua set the bar high; it was He who said that if you even look upon another with lust you have already committed adultery in your heart (see Matt. 5:28). He knows that once you start letting that lust enter into your heart, you are about to fall.

4. Agree on Your Standards

Many have good intentions but don't follow through. Here is a key to why: *"Watch and pray, lest you enter into temptation. The spirit indeed is willing, but the flesh is weak"* (Matt. 26:41). When both people in the relationships are not committed to purity, you will be pulled down.

5. Set Your Mind Back on God

So what should you do if you find yourselves already pushing that line, or worse, having gone past it? One thing that often happens with couples who begin having sex before marriage is that they stop really communicating, reading their Bibles together, and praying together. If you truly love Jesus, you'll find a way to stop. If you both truly love each other, you will find a way to stop.

The Scripture says, *"For it is better to marry than burn **with passion**"* (1 Cor. 7:9). However, rather than rushing into a marriage that may not last, I suggest that you may want to "cool it" for awhile or break up altogether in order to repent and get your heart wholly focused back on your Abba Father. This will be tough, but if you love your Savior God, pray and He will help you both to make this correction. *He* is the only one who can.

STUDY GUIDE INFORMATION

Following this, I have prepared a small study guide. It has been prepared for small group learning sessions or for personal use to help you with your spiritual learning and growth. Some may want to just read the book first and then go back to the questions later. Here are some helpful hints.

1. When you get to group, bring this book, your Bible, and your pen or pencil.

2. Most Scriptures are in the New King James Version, unless otherwise noted. Any version will work (except for fill in the blanks, but you have the Living Isaiah 54 book to follow there); however, the New King James or King James will be easiest to follow for this set of questions. If the question calls for a different version of the Bible, you may also go to www.biblegateway.com.

3. Have your assigned pages in your workbook done when it is time for group, so you can be ready to answer and discuss with others. In the "Open for Discussion" questions, there is no right or wrong answer.

4. These are lengthy chapters and study questions. It may take a couple of hourlong sessions to get through the chapter. Feel free to extend it into next week's session instead of trying to rush through.

5. Use your group sessions as a time to listen to others and for others to listen to you. This is a time of personal sharing, personal learning, and personal healing with *Jehovah-Ishi* and *Jehovah-Rapha* (your Husband and Healer). Also remember in a group setting to hold each other up in strictest confidentiality. If you are still not comfortable sharing your "deepest, darkest" with others, find a trusted friend so you can "confess and be healed" according to James 5:16.

I sincerely hope and pray that, as you work through this book, you will grow closer in your walk with your Lord and Savior and gain in your daily knowledge while serving Him and others.

STUDY GUIDE

Chapter One

GET READY TO PRAISE HIM!

"Sing O barren, you who have not borne! Break forth into singing, and cry aloud, you who have not labored with child! For more are the children of the desolate than the children of the married woman," says the Lord (Isaiah 54:1).

1. A. What are the two forms of praise used in verse one?

    1. _____
    _____
    _____

    2. _____
    _____
    _____

   B. What Scripture answers the thought, *I don't understand His ways?*

    _____
    _____
    _____

2. A. What is the Hebrew word meaning "a word in due season"?

      _____

    B. Write Isaiah 50:4 down. Then list an example of a time when you felt you were speaking the right word to someone.

      _____

      _____

      _____

      _____

3. Fill in the blanks. Romans 8:15-17:

> *For you did not receive the spirit of bondage again to _____,
> but you received the Spirit of _____ by whom we cry out,
> "Abba, Father." The Spirit Himself bears witness with our spirit
> that we are children of God, and if children, then_____ —
> heirs of God and _____ _____ with Christ...*

4. True or False? An adopted child (Gentile) bears the same heritage in God's eyes as a biological one (Jewish).

> *Enlarge the place of your tent, and let them stretch out the
> curtains of your dwellings; do not spare; lengthen your
> cords, and strengthen your stakes* (Isaiah 54:2).

5. How does the above verse speak to you? Open for discussion.

      _____

      _____

      _____

6. Fill in the blanks. Isaiah 40:31:

> But those who _____ on the Lord, shall renew their
> _____; they shall mount up with wings like _____,

they shall run and not be _____, they shall walk and not

_____.

7. The Hebrew word *chakah* means to:_____

_____.

8. In the NKJV Bible Commentary, it says,

> In Scripture, the word "wait" normally suggests the anxious, yet confident, expectation by God's people that the Lord will intervene on their behalf.

So, waiting is the working out of _____.

> *For you shall expand to the right and to the left, and your descendants will inherit the nations, and make the desolate cities inhabited* (Isaiah 54:3).

9. A. What are your "desolate cities" right now? Open for discussion.

_____

_____

_____

_____

B. What are your hopes and dreams for you and your loved ones, as you move from desolation (from your disappointments in life) to expanding to the right and left (growth)?

_____

_____

_____

_____

10. In the Bible, Deuteronomy 28 is known as the _____ chapter.

11. Fill in the blanks. Matthew 22:37-38:

Jesus said to him, "'You shall love the Lord your God with all your heart with all your soul, and with all your mind.' This is the _____ and _____ _____."

12. What is the second greatest commandment according to Yeshua?

_____

_____

_____

13. True or False? According to First Samuel 15:22, to disobey is better than sacrifice.

14. What sin is "as the sin of witchcraft"?

_____

_____

_____

15. You've heard a word from the Lord. After waiting, what are two other important words to follow?

_____

_____

_____

16. A. What tribe of the Israelites is to go "first in battle"?_____

    B. What does the name *Judah* mean? _____

17. Have you been to the Garden of Gethsemane lately? If so, bear your soul here. List how you are waiting for your Abba Father to answer.

_____

_____

_____

18. List the meanings of the names of the Lord.

*Adonai:*_____

*El Shaddai:*_____

*Elohim:*_____

*Jehovah-Rapha:*_____

*Jehovah-Shalom:*_____

*Jehovah-Jireh:*_____

19. Fill in the blanks. Yeshua took the mystery of those 39 stripes for us! Isaiah 53:5 says:

> *He was _____ for our transgressions, He was _____ for our iniquities, the chastisement of our _____[Shalom] was upon Him, and by His _____, we are_____ [Jehovah-Rapha].*

20. What is the most important gift given to us by God for our lives?

_____

_____

_____

_____

Let's Pray

Precious Father God, we give You praise, we give You glory, we give You honor this day. We rejoice and are glad, for You have given this day to us. Help us, Father, as we dive further into the study of Isaiah 54. Give us wisdom and insight. Help us to go deeper into the cracks and crevices of our lives, to come out the other side and stand richly before You. Use this to enrich our lives, Father, so we may be servants to others, just as Your precious Son, Yeshua, was and is and is to come!

We love You, Father, with all our hearts, souls, and minds. You are our Healer, our Jehovah-Rapha. You are our peace, our Jehovah-Shalom. You are our Jehovah-Jireh provider. Thank You for sending Your precious Son, Yeshua, to us for our very own salvation! Thank You for taking those 39 stripes for us! It's by the precious name of Jesus—the Lamb of God—we pray, amen!

Chapter Two

MAGNIFY HIM—NOT OUR FEAR!

Do not fear, for you will not be ashamed; neither be disgraced, for you will not be put to shame; for you will forget the shame of your youth, and will not remember the reproach of your widowhood anymore (Isaiah 54:4).

1. The above verse tells us not to fear. According to Lamentations 1:9, *who* likes to magnify himself and cause us fear?

    _____

    _____

    _____

2. Out of humble respect and submission, who are we supposed to fear?

    _____

    _____

    _____

3. Fill in the blanks. We are in a daily battle, dear hearts! First Peter 5:8-9:

    Be _____, be _____: because your

    _____ the devil walks about like a roaring lion, seeking

whom he may _____. Resist him, _____ in
the faith...

4. According to Second Timothy 1:7, God didn't give us a spirit of fear, but of what? _____ and _____ and a _____ _____.

5. What unhealthy fears have been gripping you lately? List them here and then start speaking God's Word over them! Confess and be healed! Open to discussion.

_____

_____

_____

6. Get out your Bible and look up First Corinthians 6:9-10. Let's face it; we all have committed something (maybe many things) on that list. Read verse 11. We have been cleansed, sanctified and justified in His Holy name by whom? By _____ and by the _____.

7. Fill in the blanks. "You have to get _____ before you can _____!"

8. Are you wrestling with some things right now? Please list them here and discuss.

_____

_____

_____

9. True or False? If you're wrestling against something, you are really just fighting against people.

10. Fill in the blanks. If that "spirit of fear" begins to grip you, a great verse to remember is First John 4:4:

_____ *is He* [Yeshua] *that is in* _____, *than he that is in the* _____ (KJV).

11. Fill in the blank. Fear that grips your mind is what the enemy is after! But, First John 4:18 tells us *"There is no fear in* _____*..."*

12. List some of the things you have been fearful of in the past and how you got victory over them! List the Scriptures that have helped you win the battle! Open to discussion.

_____

_____

_____

13. List four ways the enemy will try to assault you?

_____

_____

_____

14. A. If you are guilt-ridden and under condemnation, who is throwing that in your face? _____

    B. Fill in the blanks. Romans 8:1:

    There is therefore now no _____ *to those who are in* _____ _____, *who do not walk according to the* _____, *but according to the* _____.

15. Father God doesn't bring us confusion, but what? _____

16. A. In the Book of Genesis, satan made Eve "_____" and eat of the fruit.

    B. List an experience when the enemy caused you to forget what you already knew to be true!

_____

_____

_____

_____

17. Fill in the blank. Thank God that He loves you enough to correct you! *"For whom the Lord loves He corrects..."* (_____ 3:12).

18. If you don't walk in forgiveness, list some of the things that can creep into your life.

_____

_____

_____

_____

_____

19. Fill in the blanks. Hosea 10:12 advises:

Break up your fallow _____, for it is time to _____ the Lord, till _____ comes and rains righteousness on you.

20. Find out what your name means. Look it up on the Internet if you have to. Ask Father to give you a new name! (In my case, He just let me know that it didn't mean "bitter," but "Exalted of God.") List your name and the meaning here.

_____

_____

_____

_____

21. Be careful what you speak! According to Proverbs 18:21, life and death are in the power of the _____.

LET'S PRAY

Gracious and heavenly Father, thank You so much that we don't have to fear or be ashamed. Thank You for Your Word that gives us power and victory over the enemy. For You, O Lord, haven't given us that awful spirit of fear, but the spirit of Your power and of Your Love and of a precious sound mind. It is the mind of Your Son, Christ Himself, that You have given us.

Also, thank You, Father, that You are jealous for us! You love us enough to correct us to keep us out of harm's way. Help us, Lord, to forgive others, to break up our fallow ground in this area. We ask that those we have wronged can find the grace and mercy to forgive us. Give us that grace and mercy to forgive those who have wronged us as well. Thank You, Father, for giving us new names—precious names with precious meanings! Oh, how You love us, Father! We love You and thank You for seeing us through it all. It's in Your Son's precious name, Yeshua, that we pray. Amen!

Chapter Three

OUR LOVE—OUR HUSBAND

For your Maker is your husband, the Lord of hosts is His name; and your Redeemer is the Holy One of Israel; He is called the God of the whole earth (Isaiah 54:5).

1. In the above verse, Father God, our Maker is our _____ and our _____!

2. Fill in the blanks. The ancient Word applies today! Hebrews 13:8 says, *"Jesus Christ is the same _____, _____ and _____."*

3. A. Name ways you can care for your precious Husband in your single-ness. Or if you're married, name the ways you can take care of your heavenly Husband from this perspective as well.

_____

_____

_____

_____

   B. If you're a woman, how might these ways help you to learn to take care of your earthly husband (now or in the future)? If you're a man, how would these ways help you learn to take care of your wife (now or in the future)? Open to discussion.

_____

_____

_____

_____

4. Fill in the blanks. I love the intimacy our Father wants with us! The Stone Edition Tanach puts it best:

> *And it shall be on that day—the word of Hashem* [literally "_____
> _____"]—*that you will call Me Ishi* [my _____] *and you will no longer call Me Baali* [my _____]" (Hosea 2:18).

5. The term *Messianic-Jew* refers to Jews who believe in Jesus-_____, the one true _____ God, that the _____ has come.

6. A. Rabbi Moshe Laurie gives us a great quote. He said, "You have Old Testament and New Testament, but it's the _____ testament in God's eyes."

B. Rabbi Laurie noted how Yeshua treated the Church. Did Yeshua dedicate part of His life or His whole life to the Church?

_____

_____

_____

C. According to Rabbi Laurie, Messiah treated the Church with _____ and _____ and _____, even when they were wrong.

D. True or False? A husband and wife should try to please God, and through pleasing Him, they are pleasing to one another.

E. If a couple is trying to please God, there is not _____, but giving and taking _____ upon the Word of God.

F. If a husband and wife are screaming at one another and then both realize, *Hey, this isn't pleasing to God,* is it relevant who is right and who is wrong at that point? Why? Please discuss.

_____

_____

_____

"For the Lord has called you like a woman forsaken and grieved in spirit, like a youthful wife when you were refused," says *your God* (Isaiah 54:6).

7. The above verse speaks to much hurt in people's lives. Name and discuss your hurts due to a divorce or even an engagement or pre-engagement that never produced a marriage. If you've never had the above happen, think of a breakup of a past relationship.

_____

_____

_____

8. Fill in the blanks. As you bear the hurts of your past, get past them and start to look to your future! Second Corinthians 5:17:

> *Therefore if any man be in* _____, *he is a* _____
>
> _____: _____ *things are passed away; behold, all*
>
> *things are become* _____ (KJV).

9. What does the Greek word *logos* mean? _____

   _____

10. True or False? If you've been "pretty good" all your life, you really don't need to heed all the written Word of God.

11. A. Ephesians 5:26 says, *"That He might sanctify and cleanse her with the washing of water by the word..."* What does this mean in your own words?

   _____

   _____

   _____

   B. Name a time you felt the Word of God was showing you different areas in your life that you needed to clean up? Open to discussion.

   _____

   _____

   _____

LET'S PRAY

Gracious Lord, thank You for loving us so much that You want us to call You our Husband, our Redeemer, who is the Holy One of Israel. The Lord of Hosts is Your name! You want that precious intimacy with us. Teach us, Father, as we learn to be obedient to You and Your Word in our times of singleness or even loneliness, to take care of You. In doing so, You will teach us how to treat one another.

Thank You, Lord, for calling out to us, even when we have been forsaken by others. You are right there to help us at any time, Father! Help us to remember that and to cry out to You! Help us to remember that old things are passed away and that we are new creatures in Christ Jesus. You have sanctified and cleaned us by the washing of Your Word. It's in your Son's precious name we pray, amen!

Chapter Four

ONE WORD—MERCY

For a mere moment I have forsaken you, but with great mercies I will gather you (Isaiah 54:7).

1. Look up Hebrews 13:5. At first glance, it seems we have a contradiction with the above verse out of Isaiah. Since there are no contradictions in the Bible, what did Father God use to illustrate His point?

   _____

   _____

   _____

2. Have you had a recent period in your life when you were forsaken (left behind, abandoned, deserted). Please list it here and discuss.

   _____

   _____

   _____

   _____

3. Look again at the above verse. It starts out with great pain, but the next sentence changes *everything*. Write that sentence here.

    _____

    _____

    _____

4. Read Hosea 2—what I like to call the "Wilderness Chapter." Verses 6-7 speak of God hedging up your way and walling you in. What does this mean?

    _____

    _____

    _____

    _____

5. Name an experience when Father God has hedged up *your* way. Open to discussion.

    _____

    _____

    _____

    _____

6. A. Fill in the blanks. Isaiah 64:8:

    You are our _____; we are the _____, and You our _____; and all we are the _____ of Your hand.

    B. Just as pottery goes through the fiery kiln to purify and harden it, why does Father put you through a test?

    _____

    _____

    _____

7. A. Fill in the blank. The Bible speaks of a *"godly sorrow that leads to* _____ *"* (2 Cor. 7:9).

    B. What are some of the wrong thoughts and wrong issues in your heart that you need to let the Potter burn off? (Remember, if you're in a group, to keep *all* shared information strictly confidential.)

    _____

    _____

    _____

8. True or False? Our heavenly Father desires to keep feeding us milk the rest of our lives.

9. Hosea 2:14 speaks of Father God alluring us where? _____. And speaking what to us? _____. He is going to give us a door of what? _____. And what are we going to do there? _____!

10. What is our Husband Redeemer up to in Hosea 2:19-20? Tell of how this Scripture speaks to you.

    _____

    _____

    _____

    _____

11. Please list a few of your favorite definitions of the lovely word *mercy* here.

    _____

    _____

    _____

    _____

> *"With a little wrath I hid My face from you for a moment:*
> *but with everlasting kindness I will have mercy on you," says*
> *the Lord, your Redeemer* (Isaiah 54:8).

12. Name a time when, in your disobedience, you felt like Father God (with a little wrath) hid His face from you. Open to discussion.

_____

_____

_____

_____

13. True or False? The Lord, your Redeemer, will not have mercy on you during your disobedience.

> *"For this is like the waters of Noah to Me: for as I have*
> *sworn that the waters of Noah would no longer cover the*
> *earth, so have I sworn that I would not be angry with you,*
> *nor rebuke you* (Isaiah 54:9).

14. A. With God's promise to not flood the earth, who *"comes in like a flood"* according to Isaiah 59:19? _____

   B. In the Tanach version of this same verse, what does it say the Spirit of Hashem will do?

_____

_____

_____

_____

15. True or False? Confession is good for the soul! Just be careful who you confess to!

> *For the mountains shall depart and the hills be removed, but*
> *My kindness shall not depart from you...* (Isaiah 54:10).

16. Name a past experience when something or someone was removed from your life. Also name a blessing during this trial that helped you to know, in the midst of things being removed, that God was with you. Please discuss.

    _____

    _____

    _____

    _____

17. Fill in the blanks. Hebrews 4:16-17:

    Let us therefore come _____ to the throne of _____, that we may obtain _____and find _____ to help in time of need.

18. The biblical symbolism of the number seven is what? _____ and _____.

19. If you have been despised, rejected, or unfairly judged, especially by those who have boards in their own eyes, what does Scripture tell you to do? (See James 1:2.) Who are you becoming like?

    _____

    _____

    _____

    _____

    "Nor shall My covenant of peace be removed," says the Lord, who has mercy on you (Isaiah 54:10).

20. Adonai is covenanted not only to the _____ (and to us) as their _____ partner—*"Thy Maker is Thine Husband,"* but also to them as their _____.

LET'S PRAY

Dear Lord, You have gathered us with Your great mercy in our time of trials. In our wilderness, You come to woo us, teach us, and correct us by Your precious Holy Spirit. With Your precious touch, You mold us and make us as only the Master Crafter can do. Test us, purify us! We thank You for never leaving or forsaking us. Thank You for unmerited mercy and lovingkindness toward us. As our precious Husband and Peacemaker, we thank You that You have given us access boldly to Your great throne room of grace and mercy. It's in Yeshua's great name we pray, amen!

Chapter Five

THE GRACE CHAPTER

O you afflicted one, tossed with tempest, and not comforted...
(Isaiah 54:11).

1. The number five has the biblical symbolic meaning of what?
   _____

2. Name a time in your life of great affliction, when you were tossed about and not comforted, and tell how you got through it. This could be a sickness, a loss of someone you loved, or a time of great financial difficulty.

   _____

   _____

   _____

3. True or False? It is according to your works that you are saved. (See Ephesians 2:8-9.)

4. Titus 3:5-7 is a great teaching about works, mercy, washing, grace, and hope. Get out your Bible and write your version down here. Read each other's different versions aloud and then discuss this awesome verse.

    _____

    _____

    _____

5. Some Christians live by law and some by grace. Which one are you (or possibly which one were you) and why?

    _____

    _____

    _____

    _____

6. True or False? When you find one of your brothers or sisters falling back into sin, you are to strongly admonish them.

7. Fill in the blanks. *El Shaddai*—Who is Enough—tells you to:

    ...work our your own _____ with fear and trembling; for it is _____ who works in you both to will and to do for His _____ pleasure (Philippians 2:12-13).

8. Read Romans chapters 6 through 8. These are some of Paul's greatest teachings. This study could take months, but I will just make a few notes here:

    A. True or False? Grace gives us an excuse to sin!

    B. Fill in the blanks. Romans 6:12: *"Therefore do not let _____ reign in your mortal _____, that you should obey it in its _____."*

C. Look up Romans 7:15. It seems like this sentence Paul wrote is one we would all agree on and have our own struggles with (sin). What does it mean to you? Open to discussion.

_____

_____

_____

_____

D. Out of these three chapters in Romans, write out one of your favorite Scriptures. (Pick ones we haven't already used above.) It can be anything that is speaking to your heart right now, or one that has spoken to you in the past.

_____

_____

_____

9. We've come to the word *grace*. List at least three of your favorite definitions here.

_____

_____

_____

_____

10 Fill in the blanks. Proverbs 18:21:

_____ and _____ are in the power of the _____,
And those who love it will eat its _____.

11. True or False? According to Psalm 55:16-18, we can complain to the Lord!

12. Who in the Bible was blameless, upright, feared God, and shunned evil? _____

13. Fill in the blanks.

> *Thus says the Lord, the God of _____ your father: I have*
> *_____ your prayer, I have seen your _____; surely*
> *I will _____ you...* (2 Kings 20:5).

14. A. True or False? According to Numbers 21:4-9, the brass serpent was just another idol the Israelites made.

   B. True or False? According to John 3:14, the brass serpent is a representation of Yeshua being lifted up on the cross.

15. According to Second Kings 5, who was the commander of the Syrian army who had leprosy and was sent to the prophet Elisha? _____

> *Behold, I will lay your stones with colorful gems, and lay*
> *your foundations with sapphires. I will make your pinnacles*
> *of rubies, your gates of crystal, and all your walls of precious*
> *stones* (Isaiah 54:11-12).

16. A. What is the biblical gemstone meaning of sapphire?

   _____

   _____

   _____

   _____

   B. What is the symbolism of the ruby?

   _____

   _____

   _____

   C. How is the crystal or amethyst described?

   _____

   _____

_____

_____

17. True or False? We are called to be a holy priesthood of the most High God.

18. Fill in the blanks. First Peter 2:9 says,

But you are a _____ generation, a royal _____, a holy nation, His own special _____, that you may _____ the praises of Him who called you out of darkness into His marvelous _____.

19. How do First Peter 2:10 and Hosea 2:23 parallel each other?

_____

_____

_____

_____

20. True or False? You have not obtained mercy through Him who rent the veil—your Savior and Redeemer—Yeshua.

Let's Pray

Our heavenly Savior and Redeemer, thank You for the lovely gift of grace. Thank You that we don't have to earn it but You freely give it in and of Yourself. Help build our faith, Father. Thank You for the gift of Yeshua—our Salvation—who makes it so that we no longer live under law, but under grace. Thank You, El Shaddai, for helping us to work out our own salvation through fear and trembling. Help us, Lord, to bring our complaints before You, for You hear and answer our tears and prayers. You, our Husband Redeemer, are building our "spiritual house" with precious stones. We are even a royal priesthood, a chosen generation unto You, Father! What a privilege! What great Mercy You show toward us.

You are our precious Husband and Redeemer. It's in Your Son's Holy name we pray, amen!

Chapter Six

HIS PEACE; HIS RIGHTEOUSNESS

All your children shall be taught by the Lord, and great shall be the peace of your children (Isaiah 54:13).

1. The above is a promise from God. Even though you may not be seeing the fruit of it at the moment, what are the two promises that are given?

    _____

    _____

    _____

2. Your Husband and _____ feels your broken heart. He knows your _____ when your children are gone for whatever _____.

3. What Scripture tells you to *"Write the vision and make it plain on tablets, that he may run who reads it"*? _____

4. True or False? God heals the backsliders; He loves them freely.

5. Sometimes the Lord shows us hard things. Name a hard thing lately in your life. Feel free to discuss.

    _____

    _____

    _____

6. A. Fill in the blanks. The heading to Psalm 44 in the Tanach version reads, "Vividly portraying the recurring _____

and _____ of exile, Israel pleads for _____
to endure until it is redeemed."

    B. Does the above parallel your life today? What is it that you, like
the Israelites, need to pray for?

_____

_____

_____

7. Name the chapters in Ephesians where you can find many Scriptures
you can use to pray over your loved ones. _____.

8.   A. The Greek word *dunamis* means what? _____

    B. Fill in the blanks. In Ephesians 1:21 and 3:10, it speaks of *"principalities and powers."* This use of the word *power* comes from the Greek
word _____, which "denotes the _____
power...delegated influence." As in "_____ over persons,
_____, dominion, _____, rule."

9. What Scripture gives you specific authority to claim salvation over
your household?

_____

_____

_____

_____

10. Do you think any one is ever a lost cause to the Lord? Why or why not?

_____

_____

_____

_____

11. According to Galatians 5:19-22, what are some of the works that the flesh can bring?

   _____

   _____

   _____

12. According to Galatians 5:22-26, what can obedience to God's Word bring us?

   _____

   _____

   _____

13. True or False? Less than 25 percent of "born-agains" (Christians) think it is morally acceptable to have premarital sex.

14. A. Fill in the blanks. We are supposed to *"have the_____ of Christ,"* yet the Bride, His _____, has anything but! Sadly, many have adopted a "_____-view" instead of Christ's view. We need to return to our _____ love!

   B. Revelation 2:4 admonishes, *"_____, I have somewhat against thee, because thou hast _____ thy first love"* (KJV).

   C. Who is it we need to return to, fall in love with again?

   _____

   _____

   _____

15. What evil spirit can lead God's own people into sexual immorality and idol worship and even loves to control and manipulate?

   _____

   _____

   _____

16. Your body is what to the Holy Spirit?

_____

_____

17. A. If you continue in sin, what does Romans 1:28 say God will turn you over to?

_____

_____

_____

B. The Greek word for *reprobate* is *adokimos,* which means what?

_____

_____

_____

> *In righteousness you shall be established; you shall be far from oppression, for you shall not fear; and from terror, for it shall not come near you* (Isaiah 54:14).

18. Second Peter 1:3-7 tells us about the knowledge of God, who has called us by glory and virtue. What are some great things God adds to our faith if we choose to escape corruption (the world)?

_____

_____

_____

LET'S PRAY

Precious Redeemer Husband, we praise You and thank You for revealing Your Word to us today. Father, we stand on the promise that our children and our children's children will be taught by You, and their peace shall be great. We do not cease to give thanks for our loved ones, Father, and pray they may know Your love and that they be filled with the fullness of You, Father. We claim Your saving grace over our households. We claim the fruits of Your precious Spirit, oh Lord. Forgive us, Father, where we have strayed, and help us return to our first love—Your precious, Son Yeshua. Help establish us in virtue, knowledge, self-control, perseverance, godliness, brotherly kindness, and love. It's in Yeshua's name we pray, amen!

Chapter Seven

THE BATTLE

Indeed they shall surely assemble, but not because of Me. Whoever assembles against you shall fall for your sake (Isaiah 54:15).

1. A. Write down some of the battles that are assembling against you right now. Feel free to discuss.

    _____

    _____

    _____

    B. The second part of the above verse in Isaiah has a promise. What is it?

    _____

    _____

    _____

2. Fill in the blanks. The _____ _____ syndrome that all parents go _____ seems to get tweaked up a _____ when single.

Behold, I have created the blacksmith who blows the coals in the fire, who brings forth an instrument for his work; and I have created the spoiler to destroy (Isaiah 54:16).

3. Fill in the blanks. This verse sounds like preparation for war. Remember that _____ (Judah) goes first in a (_____) battle.

4. Fill in the blanks. Isaiah 42:12-13 says:

    Let them give _____ to the Lord, and declare His _____ in the coastlands. The Lord shall go forth like a _____ man; He shall stir up His zeal like a man of _____...He shall _____ against His enemies.

5. In Matthew 10:1, Jesus called His 12 disciples together. Who are His disciples today? _____

6. It's easy to get caught up in the power of _____; however, make sure you're not boasting in _____ for _____ sake.

7. According to Ephesians 6:11-13, you need to put on the whole armor of God, because you don't wrestle against flesh and blood, but against what?

    _____

    _____

    _____

8. Fill in the blanks. Ephesians 6:14 tells you about *"the belt of truth."* *Truth* comes from the Greek word _____, which means "_____ truth or the faith and practice of the _____ religion is called 'truth' either as being true in itself and _____ from the true God, or as declaring the _____ and will of the _____ true God, in opposition to the worship of false idols. Hence...to mean _____ truth, gospel _____...."

9. What definition does the Key Word Study Bible give for *righteousness?*

_____

_____

_____

10. A. Fill in the blanks. Ephesians 6:15 says, *"Having shod your feet with the preparation of the gospel of peace..."* You must prepare yourself to _____ in peace with the Word, the _____ of our Lord.

    B. Fill in the blanks. The Word itself may stir up some _____ at times from others, but be ready to be _____.

11. Fill in the blanks. Darts from the _____ are going to start _____ about when you get in the battle, but lift your _____ and have _____.

12. Fill in the blanks. Scripture tells you that *"Abraham _____ and it was accounted to him as _____"* (Rom. _____).

13. Fill in the blanks. Satan may win a _____, but the _____ of the tribe of Judah, _____ Himself, has already _____ the war!

14. According to the Bible, you war with the Word, which is what?

_____

_____

_____

15. Fill in the blanks. Ask the One who provides you with _____ to move you on and up from _____ to trust and _____. _____ will move you _____ the battle.

16. A. Fill in the blanks. James 1:5-7:

    If any of you lacks _____, let him ask of God...But let him ask in _____, with no doubting, for he who _____ *is like a wave of the sea driven and* _____ *by the wind. For let not that man supposed that he will receive anything from the Lord; he is a* _____—_____ *man, unstable in all his ways.*

B. Name some of the ways you are being tossed about at the moment and what you need to ask God for. Open for discussion.

_____

_____

_____

No weapon formed against you shall prosper, and every tongue which rises against you in judgment you shall condemn... (Isaiah 54:17).

17. *"No weapon formed against you shall prosper."* That means they're going to what? _____. But they're not going to what? _____.

18. Fill in the blanks. If you can totally _____ to Father God, if you can trust Him enough to give Him your very _____, you will be among the most prized and dangerous _____ in God's army!

19. A. Fill in the blanks. Second Corinthians 10:5:

Casting down _____ *and every high thing that* _____ *against the knowledge of God, and bringing into* _____ *every* _____ *to the obedience of Christ.*

B. Fill in the blanks. Think of every Scripture verse that becomes real to you (your _____ word), as _____ blocks. As you build up your mind with the _____ of the Lord (the Word), it delivers the final blow to the _____. _____ has already won; He did it for us!

20. Fill in the blanks. One of the gifts of the Holy Spirit is speaking in tongues. John 7:38 says, *"He that _____ on Me, as the scripture hath said, out of his belly shall flow rivers of_____ water"* (KJV).

21. In Matthew 17:21, Jesus said, *"However, this kind does not go out except by prayer and _____."*

22. Look at all the tools *Adonai* has given us to win the war! Name at least seven of them.

_____

_____

_____

_____

_____

LET'S PRAY

Father God, You are our Warrior Husband. We praise You, Father; we praise You through the battle and through our trials. We pray Your precious Words and promises to us for our children and our loved ones. We ask that You go forth like a mighty man. Go before us, Father; it is You who shall prevail against our enemies!

We put on our armor today, Father. We put on the belt of truth, and our breastplate of righteousness, having shod our feet with the preparation of the Gospel of peace. Above all, Father, help us to take up the shield of faith to be able to quench all the fiery darts of the wicked one. We take up the helmet of salvation and the sword of the Spirit, which is Your Word. For the weapons of our warfare are not carnal, but are mighty for the pulling down of strongholds!

We ask for faith, wisdom, and righteousness, which only come from You. We claim that no weapon formed against us shall prosper, and we cast down every vain imagination that exalts itself against the knowledge of You, Father. We ask that You bring every thought of ours into the obedience of Yeshua. We thank You for Your gifts from the Holy Spirit to us, Father. And we ask it all in Your precious Son's holy name, Yeshua, amen.

Chapter Eight

NEW BEGINNINGS

This is the heritage of the servants of the Lord... (Isaiah 54:17).

1. True or False? You can expect victory if you are a servant of the Most High!

2. Fill in the blanks. The number eight symbolizes _____ _____. You have come out of _____ and are now looking toward future _____.

3. Fill in the blanks. According to the Stone Edition Tanach, even Hashem says,

   For behold, I am bringing forth a _____ _____! Now it will sprout, you will surely _____ it: I will make a road in the _____ and in the wilderness rivers (Isaiah 43:19)

4. True or False? Compassion does not begin the healing process.

5. The word *save* means what? _____ _____

6. A. Fill in the blanks. Have you been wallowing a little too long in the _____, overwhelmed, anxious, and _____ on your Husband and His Word and simply choose to change your _____.

7. If you quit hoping, you have what? _____

8. Fill in the blanks. *"Be _____ and _____ that I am God..."* (Ps. 46:10). In *your _____*, in *your _____* place is where *you* will begin to _____, to know God.

   "...And their righteousness is from Me," says the Lord (Isaiah 54:17).

9. According to Isaiah 64:6, our righteousness is what? _____ _____

10. True or False? Christians can get wounded in the battle by "friendly fire."

11. Fill in the blanks. John 16:33 records Yeshua saying,

    These things I have spoken to you, that in Me you may have

    _____. In the _____ you will have tribulation; but

    be of good cheer, I have _____ the world.

12. Fill in the blanks. According to Romans 5:17, we have received an *"abundance of _____"* and the *"gift of _____"* through the One, the _____ _____—*Christ Himself.*

13. Fill in the blanks. Christ's Bride, which is representative of the _____, replies in Song of Solomon 2:16, *"My _____ is mine and I am _____."* Let that be our heart song to the _____ of our _____.

14. True or False? The Song of Solomon is where you can get a glimpse of entering the secret chamber, the throne room of God.

15. What is a Seder?

    _____

    _____

_____

_____

16. Fill in the blanks. Rabbi Laurie taught that if the Israelites would have learned early on to quit _____ (to each other about God) they wouldn't have had all the _____ they encountered. He encouraged us in _____ circumstance we are in to say, "Dayenu... It is _____."

17. A. Fill in the blanks. Israel is the _____ that is left! We are that _____ that is left! Our _____ are that remnant that is left! God always leaves a _____; that is a promise and a _____ and a future for us all.

    B. Fill in the blanks. *"Even so then, at this _____ time there is a remnant according to the election of_____"* (Rom. 11: 5).

18. True or False? God only uses perfect vessels (us) to carry on His work.

19. Fill in the blanks. The great _____ Chapter in _____ ____ speaks of those who _____ so *"...that they might obtain a _____ resurrection"* (Heb. 11:35).

20. Are you ready for a "new miracle"? What new things do you believe your Maker Husband is doing for you? Name some of the new things you would like to see happen in your life. Open to discussion.

_____

_____

_____

_____

LET'S PRAY

Our Precious Maker, our Love, our Husband—we once again come before Your throne room of grace and mercy. Thank You for victory and new beginnings! Thank You for Your compassion toward us; help us to extend that same compassion toward others. Help us, Lord, to at times just be still and know. Thank You that our righteousness is from You. Yeshua, You have overcome the world, and now we are more than overcomers! Yeshua, You are our Beloved, and we are Yours!

Teach us to say, "Dayenu—it is sufficient," as we are the remnant that is left. Use us for Your glory, Father God. Lord, we look forward to the new things You have for us. May we bring others into Your kingdom, for Your heart's desire, Father, is that not one should be lost! In Yeshua's mighty name we pray, amen!

ANSWER KEY

CHAPTER ONE

1. A. 1. singing

    2. crying aloud

    B. Isaiah 55:8: *"For My thoughts are not your thoughts, nor are your ways My ways,' says the Lord."*

2. A. *rhema*

    B. *"The Lord God has given Me, the tongue of the learned, that I should know how to speak, a word in season to him that is weary"* (Isa. 50:4). (Second part of the question is open for discussion.)

3. fear, adoption, heirs, joint heirs

4. true

5. Open for discussion.

6. wait, strength, eagles, weary, faint

7. to wait, adhere to, long, to tarry

8. hope

9. A. Open for discussion.

    B. Personal response.

10. obedience

11. first, greatest commandment

12. Matthew 22:39: *"And the second is like it: 'You shall love your neighbor as yourself.'"*

13. False

14. rebellion

15. obedience, trust

16. A. Judah

    B. praise

17. Personal response.

18. *Adonai:* Lord and Master

    El Shaddai: The All-Sufficient One

    Elohim: Our Creator

    Jehovah-Rapha: The Lord that Healeth

    Jehovah-Shalom: The Lord Is Peace

    Jehovah-Jireh: Our Provision

19. wounded, bruised, peace, stripes, healed

20. Salvation!

CHAPTER TWO

1. the enemy

2. God the Father

3. sober, vigilant, adversary, devour, steadfast

4. power, love, sound mind

5. Open to discussion.

6. Lord Jesus, Spirit of our Lord

7. real, heal

8. Open to discussion.

9. False

10. Greater, you, world

11. Love

12. Open to discussion.

13. mentally, emotionally, physically, spiritually

14. A. satan

    B. condemnation, Christ Jesus, flesh, Spirit

15. peace

16. A. forget

    B. Personal response.

17. Proverbs

18. Personal response.

19. ground, seek, He

20. Personal response.

21. tongue

CHAPTER THREE

1. Husband, Redeemer

2. yesterday, today, forever

3. A. Personal response.

  B. Open for discussion.

4. the Name, Husband, Master

5. Yeshua, living, Messiah

6. A. full

  B. His whole life

  C. compassion, mercy, kindness

  D. True

  E. compromise, based

  F. Open for discussion.

7. Personal response.

8. Christ, new creature, old, new

9. The written word.

10. False

11. A. Personal response.

  B. Open for discussion.

CHAPTER FOUR

1. He used a parable.

2. Personal response and discussion.

3. But with great mercies I will gather you.

4. Father God has put a wall up around you to keep you from getting back into an unhealthy lifestyle. He is protecting you. It is for your own good.

5. Open for discussion.

6. A. Father, clay, potter, work

B. You are like the pottery that goes under the maturing fire. The fire tests you to see if you are mature. You become cleansed, purified.

7. A. Repentance

   B. Personal response.

8. False

9. wilderness, comfort, hope, sing!

10. Personal response.

11. Tenderness of heart makes a person overlook injuries. Mercy is a distinguishing attribute of the Supreme Being. The Lord is long-suffering and of great *mercy* forgiving iniquity and transgression, and by no means clearing the guilty. Grace and favor. (These are some of my favorites. Please list yours.)

12. Open for discussion.

13. False

14. A. The enemy

   B. The Spirit of Hashem will gnaw at them.

15. True

16. Open for discussion.

17. boldly, grace, mercy, grace

18. perfection and completion

19. To count it all joy...we are just becoming more like Jesus!

20. Israelites, marriage, Peace-Maker

Chapter Five

1. grace

2. Personal response.

3. False

4. Write down Titus 3:5-7. Then share your personal response.

5. Open for discussion.

6. False

7. salvation, God, good

8. A. False

   B. sin, body, lusts

   C. Even though I know better, I do things I shouldn't do. The things I should be doing, I don't do when I should!

   D. Personal response.

9. Some of *my* favorites are: The free unmerited love and favor of God. Divine favor and influence of God in renewing the heart and keeping from sin. The application of Christ's righteousness to the sinner. Saying "grace" at the supper table! (Now you list yours.)

10. life, death, tongue, fruit

11. True

12. Job

13. David, heard, tears, heal

14. A. False

    B. True

15. Naaman

16. A. Sapphire represents hope. It is for those with sure hope in whose life and ways the please the Most High. As the color of the sky, sapphire signifies those who aspire for heavenly things and who despise all worldly matters just as if they were not on earth.

B. Ruby symbolizes preciousness. It's of great value, costly glories, wisdom, and prized treasure.

C. Crystal or amethyst represents constant thought toward the heavenly Kingdom. It represents the heart of the lowly that died with Christ. It signifies those who pray for their enemies and represents the virtue to pray for those who persecute you.

17. True

18. chosen, priesthood, people, proclaim, light

19. In both verses, it speaks of God granting you mercy even though you have not received it from others.

20. False

CHAPTER SIX

1. All your children shall be taught by the Lord and great will be their peace.

2. Redeemer, pain, reason

3. Habakkuk 2: 2

4. True

5. Personal response.

6. A. oppressions, persecutions, strength

   B. Yes, of course it does. Strength!

7. Ephesians 1 and 3.

8. A. miraculous power

   B. exousia, executive, Power, things, authority

9. Acts 16:31—*"And they said, 'Believe on the Lord Jesus Christ, and you will be saved, you and your household.'"*

10. No never! Our Husband Redeemer grants you executive power (exousia) to pray over anyone, and in Acts 16 it says your household will be saved!

11. Adultery, fornication, hatred, jealousy, selfishness, envy, murder, drunkenness, and so forth.

12. The fruits of the Spirit—joy, peace, longsuffering, kindness, goodness, faithfulness, gentleness, self-control.

13. False

14. A. mind, Church, world, first

    B. Nevertheless, left

    C. Jesus!

15. Jezebel

16. a temple

17. A. reprobate mind

    B. It means "rejected, worthless (literal and moral) and castaway."

18. virtue, knowledge, self-control, perseverance, godliness, brotherly kindness, and love.

CHAPTER SEVEN

1. A. Open for discussion.

    B. God says whoever (or whatever) comes up against you shall fall.

2. empty nest, through, notch

3. praise, spiritual

4. glory, praise, mighty, war, prevail

5. Me and you!

6. warfare, power, power's

7. Against principalities, against powers, against the rulers of the darkness of the age and against spiritual hosts of wickedness in the heavenly places.

8. *"Stand therefore, having girded your waist with the belt of truth, having put on the breastplate of righteousness, and having shod your feet with the preparation of the gospel of peace; above all, taking the shield of faith with which you will be able to quench all the fiery darts of the wicked one, And take the helmet of salvation, and the sword of the Spirit which is the word of God; praying always with all prayer and supplication in the Spirit, being watchful to this end..."*

9. alethia, divine, true, derived, existence, one, divine, truth

10. It means character, conduct, just as one should be. It means one is upright and has virtue. It also means where the heart is right with God, and means righteousness and godliness.

11. A. walk, Gospel

    B. wrath, peaceful

12. enemy, flying, shield, faith

13. believed, righteousness, 4:3

14. battle, Lion, Christ, won

15. You war with the Word, our sword.

16. strength, tears, faith, Faith, through

17. A. wisdom, faith, doubts, tossed, double-minded

    B. Open for discussion.

18. form, prosper

19. surrender, lives, warriors

20. A. imaginations, exalteth, captivity, thought

    B. *rhema*, building, Sword, enemy, Yeshua

21. believeth, living

22. fasting

23. praise, the Word (our Sword), helmet of salvation, breastplate of righteousness, Gospel of peace, belt of truth, shield of faith, prayer, angels, fasting

CHAPTER EIGHT

1. True

2. new beginnings, bondage, redemption

3. new miracle, know, desert

4. False

5. heal

6. stressed, depressed, believe, trust, countenance

7. hopelessness

8. still, know, stillness, quiet, hear

9. like filthy rags

10. True

11. peace, world, overcome

12. grace, righteousness, only One

13. Church, beloved, His, Lover, souls

14. True

15. It is the Jewish observance of the Passover, which is the remembrance of the exodus from Egypt as celebrated by Christ at the time of His Last Supper. Yeshua was and is the Passover Lamb!

16. complaining, problems, whatever, sufficient

17. A. remnant, remnant, children, remnant, hope

    B. present, grace

18. False

19. Faith, Hebrews 11, suffer, better

20. Personal response.

In the right hands, This Book will Change Lives!

Most of the people who need this message will not be looking for this book. To change their lives, you need to put a copy of this book in their hands.

> *But others (seeds) fell into good ground, and brought forth fruit, some a hundred-fold, some sixty-fold, some thirty-fold* (Matthew 13:8).

Our ministry is constantly seeking methods to find the good ground, the people who need this anointed message to change their lives. Will you help us reach these people?

> *Remember this—a farmer who plants only a few seeds will get a small crop. But the one who plants generously will get a generous crop* (2 Corinthians 9:6).

EXTEND THIS MINISTRY BY SOWING
3 BOOKS, 5 BOOKS, 10 BOOKS, OR MORE TODAY,
AND BECOME A LIFE CHANGER!

Thank you,

Don Nori Sr., Founder
Destiny Image
Since 1982

DESTINY IMAGE PUBLISHERS, INC.

"Promoting Inspired Lives."

VISIT OUR NEW SITE HOME AT
WWW.DESTINYIMAGE.COM

FREE SUBSCRIPTION TO DI NEWSLETTER

Receive free unpublished articles by top DI authors, exclusive

discounts, and free downloads from our best and newest books.

Visit www.destinyimage.com to subscribe.

Write to: Destiny Image

               P.O. Box 310

               Shippensburg, PA 17257-0310

Call: 1-800-722-6774

Email: orders@destinyimage.com

For a complete list of our titles or to place an order
online, visit www.destinyimage.com.

FIND US ON FACEBOOK OR FOLLOW US ON TWITTER.

www.facebook.com/destinyimage   **facebook**

www.twitter.com/destinyimage   **twitter**